Richard West was born in London in 1930. After Cambridge and a postgraduate year in Yugoslavia, he joined the then *Manchester Guardian*, becoming its Yorkshire correspondent. In 1958 he launched out as a freelance journalist, first in Britain and then, increasingly, on assignments abroad. A specialist on black Africa and Vietnam, he has written from almost every country in the world for publications ranging from the *Sunday Times Magazine* to the *Daily Mirror*, *New Statesman* and *Private Eye*. His books include *The White Tribes of Africa, Back to Africa* and *Brazza of the Congo*, which is due to be published this spring by Jonathan Cape. Mr West is also the author of *Sketches from Vietnam* (with drawings by Gerald Scarfe), *The Gringo in Latin America*, and *PR: The Fifth Estate*, an unloving study of the public relations business.

Industrial society is built from the raw materials supplied by the giant international mining, oil, and chemical consortia. In the first of a series of dispassionate, well-documented case-studies of how such corporations work, journalist Richard West dissects the political history of the Rio Tinto-Zinc Corporation Limited, a London-based group that today may be the largest mining company in the world.

RTZ, more than most of its competitors, supports its economic growth (the 1962/70 rate of expansion was 30% a year) by brilliant international finance. Because RTZ works with meticulous attention to detail, usually confining its activities to stable 'white' countries, its activities are generally shrouded in such discreet anonymity that certain of the more interesting details of its operations have hitherto escaped wide public notice.

Modern mining of the RTZ kind is computerized, highly mechanized, immensely technical, and conducted on an almost inconceivable scale, with movements of materials measured in hundreds of millions of tons. It entails drastic alteration of land and culture wherever it occurs, and it is these alternations, such as at Bougainville in New Guinea, that Richard West charts.

The most controversial section of this book (which covers South Africa, Rhodesia, Lesotho, South West Africa, Australia, New Guinea, and several British sites) is that dealing with RTZ's highly secret plans for mining uranium in S.W. Africa – under a South African mandate which, according to an advisory ruling of the World Court, is illegal. That uranium will be bought by the UK Atomic Energy Authority under a contract entered into despite many complications, and will also give South Africa the technical capability to build nuclear weapons.

Richard West

River Of Tears

The Rise of the Rio Tinto-Zinc
Mining Corporation

Earth Island Limited

First published 1972
by Earth Island Limited
17 Shaftesbury Avenue
London W.1.

Copyright © Richard West 1972

Jacket design by David Larkin

SBN 0.85644.002.7

Distributed by Angus and Robertson (UK) Ltd
2 Fisher Street
London W.C.1

TABLE OF CONTENTS

"I tell you, today, that every ounce of gold taken from the bowels of our soil will yet have to be weighed against rivers of tears"

(Paul Kruger, President of the Transvaal)

RIVER OF TEARS

PROLOGUE

"Here the people do not appear to know the actual cause of this permanent discolourment of the water; this river has apparently always been known as the 'rio tinto', or cloud-river. In it no kind of fish or any sort of life can exist, neither may persons, nor animals, drink of it with impunity, nor can it be utilized for any of the ordinary purposes of domestic life."
——Diego Delgado, writing in 1556 of the abandoned copper mines in south-west Spain. Quoted by W. G. Nash in *The Rio Tinto Mine. Its History and Romance.* 1904.

THE largest mining company in the world, the Rio Tinto-Zinc Corporation Ltd, is oddly obscure. Share punters favour it when the prices of metals are rising; conservationists know of its survey for copper and gold in British National Parks; the poet Robert Graves called the company "obscene". Yet many critics as well as friends do not even know that RTZ is a British company. Because of its Latin-sounding name, it is often thought to be South American. A friend of mine, one of the country's leading industrial journalists, was amazed to hear that RTZ is not a North American company. Most big British firms, such as Rolls-Royce, Whitbreads or ICI, like to promote their names and their public-relations "images" with the use of prestige advertising, by eye-catching trademarks, by sponsoring yacht races, show jumping events or places of learning. But RTZ shuns this kind of publicity. Most companies of its size have moved into big, conspicuous offices appropriate to their self-importance, such as Shell House or the Vickers or Daily Mirror buildings. In the course of writing this book I went to St James's Square where RTZ has its headquarters, and since I did not remember the actual address, I started to walk round in search. At No. 6, I stopped, feeling certain that this was RTZ——just because there was no name over the door. An old mansion, rebuilt in a blank nondescript style, it is reticent and impersonal, even a little forbidding.

This anonymity helps to explain the feebleness of the protest against RTZ's hopes of mining in the National Park. "With any other company there would have been an uproar of protest", I was told by a well-known financial writer. The Anti-Apartheid movement has paid little attention to RTZ, though RTZ has a gigantic copper mine in South Africa, an RTZ off-shoot has helped to save the economy of the Smith regime in Rhodesia, an RTZ's Rossing uranium mine, in South West Africa, has helped the South African government to build nuclear weapons.

Few Australians realize that four of the seven top companies in their country are subsidiaries of RTZ. This enormous influence has helped RTZ win a contract to mine copper and gold on the New Guinea island of Bougainville, which is run by Australia under a mandate from the United Nations. The effects of the mine on the life of the Bougainville islanders have largely escaped the attention of the British and even Australian press.

Although the British press has perforce given attention to plans by RTZ to mine in Snowdonia, it has published few reports on the same company's threats to nature in other parts of Great Britain. Its aluminium smelter on Anglesey and its lead and zinc smelter near Bristol both release potentially dangerous pollutants and have been criticized by local residents. The company is prospecting for minerals in still more of Britain's remaining unspoilt countryside, including the Scottish Highlands, the Lake District and Ulster's Mountains of Mourne.

"Taking the wealth out of the soil," says Sir Val Duncan, chairman of RTZ, "is an emotional business and it is only too easy for political and nationalistic feelings to run high."[1] These feelings can best be kept low if the public remains in ignorance of the company running the mine. And this is one of the reasons for the success of RTZ. The British think it American, the Australians think it Australian, while South Africans scarcely know of it at all.* This study of RTZ and of

---

* In Johannesburg I noticed that Rio Tinto-Zinc was sometimes confused with Lonrho, a smaller British company that has enjoyed greater publicity.

the international politics of mining is concerned with the company today. However, the present company derives from, and still has a share in, the Rio Tinto Company of Spain, the oldest surviving copper mine in the world. A brief history of Rio Tinto may help readers to understand the modern political problems of Rio Tinto-Zinc.

The massive deposits of pyrites round Rio Tinto, in south-west Spain have been mined since earliest history. The extraction of copper, the chief component of bronze, was begun before 1000 BC by the people known as Tartessians, to whose land Hercules came to carry out two of his labours. About 750 BC, the Phoenicians from Tyre and Sidon gained a monopoly over the ore and sold the metals to ancient Israel, so that the legend of King Solomon's Mines, as well as that of Atlantis, the sunken city, has been ascribed to this region. When the Phoenicians lost to Nebuchadnezzar, early in the sixth century BC, the Phocaeans, a Greek people, won the trade with Rio Tinto and the surrounding mines. The name Iberia may come from the ancient name Iber, or Iberus, for the Rio Tinto river. The name "Spania", probably given to Spain by the Phoenicians, has been attributed to a Hebrew word for people who work in mines. In the sixth century BC, the mines were captured in war by the Carthaginians, who in turn were overthrown by the Romans.

A nineteenth-century mining engineer deduced that 20 million tons of the copper slag, or waste from the smelting, near Rio Tinto dated to pre-Roman times. However, it was the Romans who first won the full wealth of the pyrites by using advanced techniques of extraction and smelting. The ores belonged to the Roman state, which leased claims and licences to prospectors, who in turn employed slaves as miners. By the end of the Republic, banking syndicates had bought out the smaller concerns to form companies with sufficient capital to exploit the deeper, more difficult ore bodies. The pit-shafts were seldom more than two and a half feet in diameter, and these primitive mines were hard to light, drain and ventilate. With neither explosives nor engines, the Romans had to depend on muscle. Although most of the miners and even the foremen and managers were slaves, local men in the Rio Tinto region could sign on for six months work. The surrounding mines were supervised by the government from a single centre at Rio Tinto, which also served as a mining school for the rest of the Empire. The government at

Rome took a detailed interest in these Spanish mines. For instance, the tyrant Tiberius ordered the murder of Marius, a proprietor at Sierra Moreno, while the reformer Flavius introduced pit-head baths.

When the Romans left, the mines were abandoned. The Moors, who ruled southern Spain until late in the Middle Ages, built exquisite cities like Cordoba and Seville, in which fine workmanship was done in copper, but they did not get any metal from Rio Tinto.

The contraction of world trade after the fall of the Roman Empire killed the market for copper. When pumping stopped, the workings and often the pumping equipment were flooded; the drainage outlets were blocked and the tunnels caved in. The traditional mining skills died out in the local population. It has been estimated that during these centuries when the mines were neglected, about 70,000 tons of metallic copper were carried into the sea by the Rio Tinto——the "tinted river". But in more than a thousand years, the countryside round the Rio Tinto did not recover from the effect of the fumes from the ancient smelters. No vegetation grew and no birds sang among the abandoned pit-shafts. A writer in 1634 described Rio Tinto's "terrorizing aspect, a simple glance at it causing apprehension and dismay to the casual and infrequent visitor".[2]

In the sixteenth century, Spain was free from the Moors; she ruled an empire in the Americas and was fighting wars in Portugal and the Low Countries. The need to finance these ventures encouraged a mineral rush at home. The discovery of a successful lead and silver mine at Guadalcanal (near Seville) led Philip the Second, in 1556, to commission a survey of known and likely ore deposits. The chief of the commission appointed a priest, Diego Delgado, to study the hills and ancient mines of Rio Tinto, which by now was part of Huelva Province. In one cave, high as a church, Delgado found shafts and tunnels as well as "a vein of mineral half-hidden by the earth which had evidently been intentionally thrown upon it to conceal it". He dug into the hillside from which he took twenty-five pounds of ore as a sample. He studied the coloured deposits left on the banks of the Rio Tinto and noted another property of the water: "if iron be placed in it, in a few days the iron disappears; this I proved".[3]

In his letter to Philip, Father Delgado asked "that in order that I may the better and more effectually serve you in this important

charge, I pray you grant me means, for I am a priest and not pos-
sessed of any means or income".[4] Perhaps Philip and his ministers
thought that Delgado had fantasized the wealth of the Rio Tinto
mine in order to wheedle money out of the Royal coffers. The Chancellor of the Exchequer ignored the repeated letters and the requests
for a grant to continue prospecting. On the side of Delgado's last
letter, the King wrote briefly: "He is dead. This may be sent to Don
Francisco in order that he may examine into the matter and advise
me if the place or mine is as alleged."[5]

In the seventeenth century, a newly created Council of Mines once
more called for surveys of Rio Tinto. One report suggested that
copper might be sent to Seville, whose foundry manufactured artil-
lery, shot, bells and other articles using copper alloyed with tin. A
licence issued in 1661 suggested using the Rio Tinto river to turn
"iron into copper by placing it into that water". This was the origin
of the process of "cementation", which proved profitable to the mine
in the nineteenth century——and damaging to the surrounding
countryside.

For nearly two centuries, Spanish governments and entrepreneurs
wanted to reopen the old Roman copper mines at Rio Tinto. Always
these efforts were baulked by bureaucracy and by the physical problems of draining the flooded pits. The modern history of the mine
began with a Swede, Liebert Wolters, who floated a joint stock
company in 1725 to raise the capital for the venture. From the start
he encountered the enmity and suspicion that all mining companies,
including the modern RTZ, are liable to encounter when they operate
abroad. Indeed Wolters, a greedy and tactless man, seems to have
gone out of the way to annoy his host country, Spain. In the prospectus for the company, in which he awarded himself 700 free shares,
Wolters claimed that an early German mine in south Spain had been
deliberately flooded by Philip the Second, out of jealousy of its
wealth. Not surprisingly, Wolters's prospectus provoked a number of
pamphlets by Spanish journalists who called him a swindler, liar and
heretic. Nevertheless Wolters raised £2,000 (a tidy sum by today's
values), of which he spent part on sending a mining expert to Rio
Tinto to supplement the meagre information contained in the fund-
raising prospectus. The expert's optimistic report caused a scramble
among the shareholders and their friends to get well-paid jobs on the

company. Jealous quarrels broke out and soon the capital had been dissipated before even an ounce of ore had been mined. After Wolters's death in 1727, the Rio Tinto contract passed into the hands of an Englishwoman, Lady Mary Teresa Herbert, who was powerful in Madrid financial and diplomatic life. A nephew of Wolters and other original shareholders sued Lady Mary and eventually won back the lease of the mine in 1746. The company struggled on in spite of persistent annoyances from the government and the local town of Zalamea, which wanted to take over the company.

At the start of the nineteenth century, the Rio Tinto mine was the only one still working in Huelva Province. It too closed in 1810 as a consequence of Napoleon's occupation. When the French commander arrived at the mine he found a mere six tons of copper. For the next fifteen years, the mine was only intermittently worked, while the unfortunate miners roved as mendicants through Huelva Province. Due to the poisoning of the soil by fumes from the smelters, it was impossible to grow food or to raise livestock and fowls as an alternative source of income. The poet Byron is said to have visited Rio Tinto during this period and to have been inspired by it to the reflection——

The dust we tread upon was once alive. . . .

Almost everybody that came to the region was shocked by its physical desolation.

The revival of mining in south-east Spain, on a scale even greater than under the Romans, was caused by the growing demand for copper. Once used mainly for coinage and ornamental work, the metal had gained new industrial uses, including brass for precision parts, but still more as a conductor for electricity. The installation of an electric telegraph on the London and North-Western Railway in 1837 marked the start of a copper boom. The Parys mines in Anglesey, which had once dictated the world price of copper, were no more capable of meeting the new need than were the vast but inaccessible ore bodies of Chile. Mining promoters knew of the great reserves of copper in Huelva Province, but these were the property of the Spanish government, which was too weak to exploit its own resources. The exploitation of the historic mines was left to the French in the 1850s and later, increasingly to the British. As the modern historian,

S. G. Checkland, points out: "Thus it was that Spain, formerly the greatest of European colonizing nations, became itself, from the mid-nineteenth century, so far as mineral resources were concerned, a colonial appendage of northern Europe."[6] As will be seen in the second part of this book, the Australians, once the world's greatest miners, have also become such a colonial appendage——and to a large extent of the same British company, Rio Tinto-Zinc.

The first ancient mines to be re-opened were those near Tharsis west of Rio Tinto. The French engineer Ernest Deligny was told by his goat-herd guide that the mines had been quite worked out in ancient times. He discovered, to the contrary, that the Romans had scarcely touched the deeper ore bodies, and had not bothered with ore of less than 4 percent copper. Moreover Deligny had learned from the Spanish at Rio Tinto their cheap and simple method of "artificial cementation" by which the pyrite ores were burned in open-air mounds, that fumed for as long as six months. It did not worry Deligny that the sulphur passed from the pyrite into the atmosphere as sulphuric acid, poisoning all vegetation for miles around.

In the 1860s the British discovered a new technique for extracting sulphuric acid from pyrites instead of from traditional brimstone. Sulphuric acid was an important requisite of the British alkali makers who provided the raw material for glass and hard soap. When the French Tharsis company ran into trouble in 1865, a group of Glasgow alkali makers offered to take them over to found the Tharsis company. Although the chief interest of the founders had been the sulphuric acid obtainable from the pyrites, the Tharsis mine was also the world's largest producer of copper. But not for long. Within less than ten years it was challenged and then outstripped by a new Rio Tinto Company.

The Tharsis Company had proved the enormous profits obtainable by large scale mining backed by sufficient capital, assured markets, a railway and modern extractive methods. In 1872, holding top place in the world production of copper and sulphur, the Tharsis Company paid a whacking 40 percent dividend. Other north European financiers were eager to get a share of the Spanish mineral wealth. The most tempting prospect was around Rio Tinto but these lodes were still being worked, however lethargically, by the Spanish Government. Far from having the capital to exploit the mines on a modern industrial scale, Spain was deep in default on its foreign loans and was under continual pressure from London bondholders.

The Tharsis Company had been formed by a group of British provincial industrialists. The purchase and exploitation of Rio Tinto required the greater resources of a group of London and foreign financiers. This group, headed by Hugh Matheson, chairman of Messrs. Matheson, of Lombard Street, London, also included Messrs. Clark and Punchard, railway contractors, Herr L. G. Dyes, a Bremen banker, and Henry Doetsch, a Spanish businessman. But what began as an international company was soon to become almost entirely British.

In February 1873, the Spanish National Assembly authorized the sale of the Rio Tinto mine, which was promptly bought by the group for £3,850,000. The principals then resold to a newly formed company, registered under limited liability, thereby clearing £150,000 in cash and £850,000 worth of shares in the new company. The muck-raking journalist Henry Labouchere denounced the group as fraudulent promoters, but the British public was eager for Rio Tinto shares.

The purchase of Rio Tinto by this powerful foreign group was a blow to the nearby Tharsis Company. The price of sulphur dropped by half and there was no longer a seller's market for copper. But in 1878 the two big companies and other smaller producers set up the first of a series of price rings. The man who negotiated this agreement, which bumped up the price of sulphur from fivepence to sixpence a unit, was paid £6,000 by Rio Tinto and correspondingly smaller sums by Tharsis and other producers. A renewed world demand for copper during the 1880s gave these mines the assurance of prosperity, even without fixing prices. By 1884, Rio Tinto had grown into the greatest mining company in the world, with 30,000 employees and an annual output of 12,668 tons of copper.

Rumours of financial malpractice dogged the Rio Tinto Company in the nineteenth century. There were many suggestions that officers of the company used inside information to speculate in mineral shares. One of the early critics of the company was Dr. Ernest Morrison, a young Australian, who was hired in 1888 as assistant medical officer to the mine. His employer, Hugh Matheson——"a pietistical Presbyterian elder"——hoped that Morrison would perform his duties well and would "help bring the word of Grace to the heathen in Rio Tinto". But humbug did not impress Dr. Morrison, who was to make a famous second career as *Times* correspondent in Peking. He described Rio Tinto as a "God-forsaken spot" which had been devastated for miles around by sulphur fumes from the mines. Resigning in August 1889, he wrote:

> I was thankful to leave Rio Tinto. . . . The immediate cause of my resignation was this: As head of the medical service, I had discovered an extensive series of frauds in the druggist department involving several thousands of pounds. On sending the Company a report on this fraud, I received an astonishing letter . . . expressing the gravest disapproval of the directors at the unbecoming language in which my report was couched. I resigned two hours after getting the letter. It appears that the frauds I discovered were insignificant compared with other frauds that soon after came to light, of which even some of the directors who had admonished me had not been guiltless.[7]

During his stay at Rio Tinto, Morrison did not bother to bring "the word of Grace to the heathen", unless to his Spanish mistress. The town of Rio Tinto was rough even compared to other mining communities: in one period of six weeks there were seven murders; and a bull-ring, the centre of vice had eventually to be bought out and razed to the ground by the company.

To answer its critics, then as now, the Rio Tinto Company encouraged friendly publicity. One early example is a book *The Rio Tinto Mine. Its History and Romance*, which first appeared in 1904. The author, William Giles Nash, fails to convey much romance, but his history of the mine is revealing. His heroes are those Anglo-Saxons, from Wolters down to the time he wrote, whose skill and efforts were spent on extracting ore. His villains are sly, lazy, bigoted Spaniards who grudge the wealth of their soil to the foreigners. In one lyrical passage, Nash advances the argument, so often repeated today, that mining brings nothing but benefit to the people of a country.

> The wretched efforts of the Spaniards themselves have been well described, in bitter terms, by a late writer, and he eloquently

endeavoured to arouse a sense of the importance and necessity of a greater national interest being taken in mining and metallurgy, and lamented the want of progress and application of his countrymen. ... Strike out from the catalogue of social progress the art of extraction of metals from the interior of the earth, and you at once eliminate the patron of development in science, art, and commerce. Interrogate History as to what has been the influence of mining and metallurgy, and she will furnish an endless list of reply and instance. She will tell you that the extraordinary civilization of Greece was but the outcome of the genius of Cadmus and of the art of working in blueing, smelting and refining metals; that the progress and great prosperity seen today in Bilbao or other industrial cities of the peninsula is but the direct result and fruit of that great industry whose germs were thrown upon the coast of Iberia by the intrepid merchants of Tyre and Sidon; that Athens owed her decadence to the laws of Lycurgus prohibiting the exploration of mines and the pursuit of the mechanical arts; whilst, again, Sparta owed her prosperity to the help and protection she afforded to them.[8]

From the beginning of the twentieth century, the Rio Tinto Company suffered from labour troubles. Anarcho-syndicalism was strong throughout Andalusia and made a special appeal to the miners, whose three major grievances against Rio Tinto were the dismissals caused by labour saving machinery, bad wages, and (worst of all) the substitution of money payment by food, or "truck". Constant agitation and stoppages came to a head in April 1920 when Rio Tinto miners struck for three weeks; in July of the same year, they struck for twelve weeks. These strikes, followed by sackings, caused further bitterness and encouraged left-wing militancy. As Spain in the early 1930s was rocked by political tremors, the Huelva mines became a stronghold of the Republicans. Many were imprisoned after a foiled rebellion in 1934. After the general election of February 1936, when the Popular Front came to power, a spokesman of Rio Tinto complained that "the company was compelled not only to re-employ the men who had been imprisoned ... but others who had been dismissed for various reasons, the most important of which was lack of employment for men of that type".[9]

When Civil War broke out in July 1936, the province of Huelva
stayed loyal to the Republic while most of southern Spain took the
side of Franco's insurgents. On Sunday, 10 July, fourteen lorry-loads
of Rio Tinto men, armed with rifles and dynamite, set out for Seville,
where they were intercepted and routed by Francoite Civil Guards.
By mid-August, the Franco forces had overcome all Republicans in
the Huelva Province, afterwards executing hundreds of miners. The
fortunes of the company changed abruptly during these violent
events. Before the general election, Rio Tinto shares stood at a high
of £22. In the beginning of August, when the mines were occupied by
Republicans, the shares had dropped to £13. With the arrival of
Franco's troops later that month, the shares rose to £30. Although
the Company favoured Franco, it did not profit much from his victory. In order to pay for German arms, Franco ordered Rio Tinto (and
other mines in the area he controlled) to ship 80,000 tons of ore to
the "Franco wharf" at Hamburg. This was providential for Hitler's
re-armament programme, since Britain and France had stopped him
getting vital ore from Sweden and other usual suppliers. The Rio
Tinto Company acquiesced to these shipments although they were
paid for in devalued pesetas.

The Second World War and the closing of most markets prolonged
the depression at Rio Tinto. The boom in copper and sulphur which
began in the late nineteen-forties only encouraged Spanish capitalists
to win back control of the mine from the foreigners. They had the
support of the Government, which wanted to use Spain's strong selling position to keep up the price of sulphur. The Company argued
that an artificially high price would encourage buyers to look for
other sources than pyrites for their supply of sulphuric acid. "The
relationship between the company and the Spanish government was
at a low ebb," recalls Roy W. Wright, deputy chairman of RTZ, "and
it took some years to demonstrate to that Government that we were
working for Spain as well as ourselves."[10] In 1954, the Rio Tinto
Company hived off its Spanish mines into a new local company of
which it sold two-thirds to a consortium of Spanish banks and the
Spanish public, for a total of £8 million. The Rio Tinto Company,
since merged into RTZ, still holds a one-third share in the Spanish
company, for whom it also supplies many managers and mining en-
gineers. But Spain today is an insignificant outpost of RTZ. The £8

million received from the Spanish consortium was used to establish a mining empire stretching across five continents.

The assets of Rio Tinto in 1954 included the £8 million from the sale to Spain; a holding in Northern Rhodesian copper; and the lively intelligence of its young chief executive, Val Duncan (since knighted). The present Chairman of RTZ had come to Rio Tinto in 1950 by way of a legal training, a job with the post-war Control Office for Germany and Austria, and two years with the National Coal Board as assistant director of marketing. After supervising the sale of the Spanish mine, Duncan sold the holdings in Northern Rhodesia, which was suffering at that time from political unrest, prior to independence. Instead, Duncan ordered prospecting in what he regarded as more stable parts of the Commonwealth such as Australia, South Africa and Canada. It was in Canada that Rio Tinto pulled off its first major success by purchasing an obscure company, Preston Mines, from which it captured a major part of Canada's new uranium industry. This was the first example of Duncan's instinct for buying into a mineral just on the eve of a boom. With the same instinct and same disregard for conventional mining wisdom, Duncan opened the Palabora copper mine on a site that had been turned down by the great South African companies. It was as if an Englishman were to open a Chinese restaurant in Hong Kong. During this period Duncan bought a uranium mine in Australia, and extended his North American interests to the United States. By the early 1960s, Rio Tinto wanted to turn to iron ore and bauxite, especially in Australia, where it found a willing partner in Consolidated Zinc.

Conzinc was a British company whose mining interests were preponderantly in Australia. The biggest Australian lead and zinc producer, Conzinc had found bauxite and had recently got a share in an aluminium smelter. It had two more smelters in Britain. Its merger with Rio Tinto in 1962 was useful to both parties. Consolidated Zinc, thanks to its strong Australian connections, had the openings for investment. Rio Tinto, thanks to uranium contracts, had the cash to invest. The newly created RTZ, with Duncan as managing director, soon acquired its present commanding position in Australian iron ore, bauxite, and aluminium and eventually in New Guinean copper. In eight years after the merger, the turnover and profits (before tax) of RTZ increased by an average of 30 percent annually. Although

1970 and 1971 were bad years due to the world drop in metal prices, RTZ has continued to expand. It is prospecting in many regions of Britain and Northern Ireland. It has continued its negotiations with the Soviet Union over a nickel mine in the Urals. It has even announced plans to prospect in such "third world" states as Brazil and Indonesia. And it now controls (assuming a price not above $10 a pound) between 15 and 20 percent of the world's uranium reserves.

The success of RTZ has been well explained by its Vice-Chairman Roy Wright, in an interview in Johannesburg: "The Rio Tinto-Zinc company has developed an unusual method of financing its worldwide mining and industrial ventures. After thorough investigation, the corporation launched large mining projects, invariably with international partners, mainly financed by foreign loans."[11] Indeed the *Economist* has described the company as "a sort of merchant bank, using its knowledge of the ways and workings of international finance to get the money for mining".[12] It gets this money because the international financiers respect the company's knowledge of mining——and of politics. As Sir Val Duncan has said: "We are very politically minded in RTZ, not party politically minded, but on an international basis."[13] Although the company has preferred to work in countries with white, stable, conservative governments, notably Canada, Australia, the United States and South Africa ——even in these countries, it has defended itself against economic nationalism by offering shares to the host country.

The brain behind RTZ in its mining, financial, above all political ventures is that of Sir Val Duncan. His name does not appear in the press as often as those of (for example) Lord Stokes or Arnold Weinstock. His gift for anecdote one must accept on trust, for there is no printed evidence to prove it. His speeches on British industry or on the need to join the Common Market are unoriginal and unmemorable. One gets the feeling that Duncan, like RTZ, prefers to appear colourless, camouflaged, in the shadow. But those who meet him in business regard him with awe. Many times while doing research for this book, I have heard Duncan described as the cleverest/ablest/shrewdest most brilliant businessman in Britain. "The trouble with the Rio Tinto-Zinc Corporation," wrote Berry Ritchie, then Mining Editor of *The Times*, "is it looks too good to be true. . . .

It has a dynamic management with a defined philosophy of direction and responsibility. You can argue it is almost patriotic to own shares in RTZ. . . . There is something almost indecent, not quite British, about the enthusiasm he [Sir Val Duncan] generates in RTZ."[14]

Undoubtedly Duncan is an able businessman. Undoubtedly RTZ is a well-run company which has made and will continue to make much money for its employees and investors. But this book is not a study of the internal workings of RTZ; still less about mining methods; least of all about mining finance. It is a study of RTZ and the politics of mining: that is, the effect of the company on the countries and societies where it operates. Even here I have been selective. RTZ is active in all five continents. I have chosen three particular regions to illustrate the different kinds of political problems that the company has to face.

Part One examines the company in southern Africa. Chapter One deals with the great Palabora mine* in South Africa itself; Chapter Two with Rhodesia; Chapter Three with Lesotho, a nominally independent state; and Chapter Four with South West Africa, which is ruled illegally by South Africa. This Part is therefore concerned with the politics of mining in countries with racial problems.

Part Two examines RTZ in Australia and New Guinea. Here the company's commanding position in local economic life has been criticized by nationalist politicians. The first three chapters deal with RTZ's exploitation of three ores——uranium, iron and bauxite (aluminium ore). The fourth and by far the longest chapter describes the effects of the company's copper mine at Bougainville, a small and once beautiful island in New Guinea, which is ruled by Australia under United Nations mandate.

Part Three examines RTZ in Great Britain. The first two chapters describe the effects of the RTZ smelters at Bristol and Holyhead. In both places the company has created jobs at a cost, so critics allege, of damage to the environment. Chapter Three tells how RTZ has been pursuing mineral prospects in Snowdonia.

* In both Palabora Mining Co. and Anglesey Aluminium Co. Ltd., RTZ has a dominant but not a majority interest.

NOTES

1. *Sunday Times*, 12–3–67.
2. W. G. Nash, *The Rio Tinto Mine*, p. 4.
3. Nash, p. 59.
4. Nash, p. 55.
5. Nash, p. 64.
6. S. G. Checkland, *The Mines of Tharsis*, p. 65.
7. Quoted in Cyril Pearl's *Morrison of Peking*, pp. 259–60.
8. Nash, pp. 47–8.
9. Franz Jellinek, *The Civil War in Spain*, p. 224.
10. *The Multinational Company* (RTZ booklet).
11. Johannesburg *Star*, 28–2–67.
12. *Economist*, 17–6–67.
13. *The Times*, 16–6–67.
14. *The Times*, 16–6–67.

Part One

SOUTHERN AFRICA

1. SOUTH AFRICA

Do not talk to me of gold, the element which brings more dissension and unexpected plagues than benefits in its train. Pray to God, as I am doing, that the curse connected with its coming may not again over-shadow our dear land, as it has come to us and our children. Pray and implore Him, who has stood by, that He will continue to do so, for I tell you, today, that every ounce of gold taken from the bowels of our soil will yet have to be weighed against rivers of tears, and the life blood of thousands of our comrades in the defence of that same soil from the lust of others, yearning for it solely because it has the yellow metal in abundance.

Paul Kruger, President of the Transvaal, quoted in *The Afrikaners* by John Fisher.

SIR VAL DUNCAN, chairman of Rio Tinto-Zinc, told the Institute of Directors on 8 July 1968: "Speaking as one who has spent all his business life in forging links between Commonwealth countries by means of natural resource developments, you can well imagine that I believe in the enduring value of the Commonwealth concept, and that the welfare and prosperity of the countries of the Commonwealth is something about which I feel deeply."[1] This claim by Sir Val is certainly true when applied to his company's interests in Canada and Australia. Its relevance to Africa is less clear. The Republic of South Africa, in which RTZ runs one of the richest copper mines in the world, was expelled from the Commonwealth in 1961 because its apartheid system offended other Commonwealth countries. Britain's decision to send arms to South Africa has so offended black African nations that the continued existence of the Commonwealth is now in doubt. Disgust with the policies of the South African government is strong even in white Commonwealth countries such as Canada and Australia (which banned a tour by South Africa's Springbok cricket team). It is true that RTZ does business with Lesotho, an African state in the Commonwealth, but Lesotho is surrounded and in part controlled by South Africa. Besides the RTZ group does even more business in South West Africa (a territory held illegally by South Africa); and in Rhodesia——a rebel, racist ex-colony of Great Britain——Rio Tinto (Rhodesia) is a bulwark of the economy. In this chapter I shall suggest that RTZ's role in Africa, far from benefiting the Commonwealth countries, gives moral and financial support to their enemies in South Africa.

For almost a century, British mining companies have played a big part in the history of South Africa. In the early nineteenth century, the Afrikaners, of Dutch extraction, migrated from the Cape (their original home) to the Transvaal and the Orange Free State, many hundred miles to the northeast. They were a pastoral people who wanted land to farm and freedom to practise their dour, psalm-singing religion. The Englishmen in the Cape had a more lenient faith and a preference for commerce rather than farming. The discovery of diamonds at Kimberley, close to the Orange Free State, enticed a swarm of Englishmen to the site. The Afrikaners, who had won partial sovereignty from the British, were still more dismayed by the discovery of gold near Johannesburg in the late 1880s. They tried in vain to stop the onrush of "uitlanders", or foreigners, including drunkards, adulterers, prostitutes, Jewish traders and Chinese laundrymen. The hatred felt by the pious Boer farmers for English and Jewish capitalists is expressed by Kruger's prophecy at the beginning of this chapter. Even Winston Churchill, a champion of the "uitlanders", was to describe Johannesburg as "Monte Carlo, superimposed on Sodom and Gomorrah". As friction grew between Afrikaners and Uitlanders, Rhodes and the mining financiers plotted to crush the remaining liberties of the Transvaal and Orange Free State. The Jameson Raid, in 1896, an act of war against the Boer republic, was paid for and organized by Rhodes's mining company. The plot failed and was later exposed, but three years later the Boer War broke out between British and Afrikaners. As Kruger had prophesied, thousands died defending their land "from the lust of others, yearning for it solely because it has the yellow metal in abundance".

The Afrikaners were not alone in disliking the gold and diamond companies. In the first decade of this century, socialist and trade union feeling spread among white English miners, many of whom were of Cornish origin. For these men, protecting their standard of living meant stopping their jobs being done by the blacks at lower rates of pay. A dispute broke out in 1907 when the management of the Knights Deep Mine ruled that one white man would in future manage three drills instead of two, a change that reduced the ratio of white overseers to native miners. Four years later, Jan Christian Smuts brought in a Mines and Works Bill, guaranteeing the white men's privileges. In spite of this, more strikes followed in 1913, when the mine owners brought in black men as "scabs", and the white miners burned down the premises of the *Star*, which was, even then, an organ of English liberal capitalism. In the subsequent fighting, 21 people were killed.

When gold prices fell after the First World War, the mine owners tried to save money by bringing in cheap black labour. In January 1922 the Government crushed the Transvaal strikers with 13-inch guns and armoured cars. For the first time the Labour Party was joined in militant action by members of the Nationalist Party, the Afrikaner die-hards who are now in power in South Africa. English-speaking socialists and Afrikaner nationalists united in fear of a threat to their livelihood from the black man (Bantu). Even the South African Communist Party condoned attacks on the black miners' compounds. Since many mine-owners were Jews, many white miners became anti-semitic as well as anti-black and anti-capitalist. This radical, working-class racialism persists to this day in the white trade unions.

But the leadership of the Nationalist Party, which came to power in 1948, no longer regards the mines as a threat to Afrikanerdom. Although many great mineowners have been English or Jewish by origin, and liberal in political views, the revenue from mining exports enables the Nationalist government to maintain an *apartheid* state in defiance of the world. It has been truly remarked in a *Times* special report on South Africa [italics added]:

Without mining, South Africa would not exist as a rich, powerful, industrial state *and indeed might not exist at all*. Only the wealth from its mines——gold, diamonds, platinum, copper, manganese, iron and coal——makes it self-sufficient. Without these minerals, its adverse balance of payments would be completely untenable.[2]

And without these minerals the South African Government could not afford armed forces equipped with the latest weapons, aircraft and ships, nor multitudinous secret policemen, with which to enforce its rule.

The RTZ copper mine at Palabora in northern Transvaal contributes much to South Africa's balance of payments. Its contribution to RTZ is more striking still. Although RTZ holds only a 39 percent share of the equity capital in the venture, RTZ's profits from the mine in 1967 were £14 million, more than its profits from all its other mines in the world. Even when copper prices are low, as they were for instance in late 1971, the Palabora mine still turns an appreciable profit for RTZ——and for South Africa's balance of payments.

The role of RTZ has been criticized by foes of the South African Government. Members of anti-apartheid groups in Britain have bought RTZ shares in order to voice their protests at Annual General Meetings. Replying to one of these questions after the meeting in May 1971, Sir Val argued that, "it was possible to find fault with the internal policies of many countries, both inside and outside Africa, but it was not RTZ's business to engage in politics." He thought it more important to carry out profitable operations which brought benefit to mankind generally and which gave a local population technical training, employment and better living standards; he pointed out that all races at Palabora enjoyed higher living standards than in the rest of Southern Africa.[3] According to another reporter, "Sir Val gave a virtuoso performance debating with the shareholding anti-apartheid demonstrators at the meeting. Always polite, cogent and incisive, he left the field victorious."[4]

Sir Val may have won his debate with the dissident RTZ shareholders; their case, when presented at greater length, is not so lightly dismissed.

There is no need to repeat at length the arguments against the apartheid system, whose injustices and cruelties are widely known to the rest of the world: the removal from Africans of all political and some legal rights, the pass system, the resettlement of Africans so that they now occupy only 13 percent of the country's land, the ban on mixed marriages, on most forms of mixed social intercourse, even on mixed laundries. Those who have been to South Africa know the atmosphere of resentment, sadness and fear that pervades that country. A poll conducted last year by two university lecturers on behalf of an Afrikaner and Nationalist newspaper showed that 90 percent of urban Africans said there was *no* "general feeling of good will between white and non-white" in the Republic. In reply to a question "If you had a choice, where (including South Africa) would you like to live?" only 21 percent named their own country, South Africa. The man most admired by those who answered the poll was Kenneth Kaunda of Zambia, followed by Nelson Mandela (who is in prison), Sir Seretse Khama (the President of Botswana), and Helen Suzman, MP (the most famous white opponent of the apartheid system).[5] Even the public relations men of the South African Government do not pretend that it is popular with the Africans. In the same way, those British politicians and businessmen who advocate close ties with South Africa, often profess to dislike apartheid, and indeed claim to be helping the blacks. They have two main arguments to support this claim:

1. That foreign investment provides well-paid jobs for the Africans, who consequently live better than black workers in other parts of Africa (or "southern Africa" to use Duncan's interesting qualification).

2. That foreign investment will lead to political progress for the Africans.

Let us examine the first argument. The whites of South Africa account for less than 19 percent of the population but they receive 74 percent of the country's total income. The difference in earnings is most marked of all in the mining industry, whose white workers are organized in a militant union dedicated to keeping the difference. Although the Africans are legally allowed to form a trade union, they are not allowed to take any industrial action. Any contravention of this law could lead to instant arrest and a fine of up to £500, imprisonment of up to three years, or both. Only white miners have pension funds and family sickness benefits. The free board and dormitory lodging provided for the blacks is calculated in their total earnings,

B

therefore constituting part payment in truck. The following figures, taken from the South African 1970 census, show annual average cash earnings in three major industries (figures in Rands):

	Whites	Coloureds	Asians	Africans
Manufacturing	3668	883	929	628
Construction	3904	1315	1805	599
Mining	4330	902	1187	220

Africans are particularly ill paid in mining because they are barred from even the semi-skilled jobs they could get in manufacturing and construction. In some industries the ratio between white and black earnings is static or narrowing, but in mining the ratio is increasing. Taking monetary incomes alone, the ratio of white to black miners' wages was about 11:1 in the mid-thirties; 18:1 in 1968; and 20:1 in 1970.[7] It has been estimated by Dr. Francis Wilson (Lecturer in the Department of Economics at Cape Town University) that in real terms, the cash wages earned by Africans in the gold mines are no higher now, and indeed probably lower, than they were in 1911.[8]

Faced by these statistics, white South Africans often reply that the blacks are nevertheless better off than those in independent Africa. Even this argument does not stand up to the facts. The following statistics, prepared by the World Bank in 1971, compare the average annual income per capita in certain African countries.[9]

Country	Per capita annual income $US
South Africa (all races)	375
Ghana	187
Senegal	162
Liberia	137
Zambia	137
South Africa (Africans only)	105
Tanzania	75
Nigeria	75
Mozambique	75
Kenya	75
Malawi	25
Portuguese Guinea	25

While I would question the worth of some of those estimates (especially that of Liberia), they are probably right to suggest that the blacks are worse off in South Africa than in Ghana and Zambia, where, according to white South African propaganda, the populations are starving. Statistics show that even in Botswana, a nearby country incomparably less rich in natural wealth than South Africa, the wages are at least as good.

It should be stressed that these comparisons refer to money income. They do not take into account the social, moral and physical degradation suffered by black South Africans——especially in the mines. For example, the South African Government thinks it undesirable that black miners should "settle" and take permanent jobs in the vicinity. Migrant labour is therefore brought in from tribal areas or from poor neighbouring countries such as Lesotho, Mozambique and Malawi. These miners have to spend two years in barracks, sleeping on concrete bunks, without the company of their wives and families. Some mine owners claim that this chaste, military atmosphere disciplines the miners and stops them being distracted from their work.

In recent years there has been agitation to ease the restrictions on black labour in South Africa. This has come not from the blacks themselves, who are not allowed to agitate, nor from the white miners, who fight any proposed change, but from the mining companies who face a shortage of skilled labour. In June 1971, Dr. A. A. Maltitz, president of the Chamber of Mines of South Africa, appealed to the white mine worker "to take a step or two up the ladder of responsibility and allow the non-white to do the same——the white man would assume a more supervisory role and would release to the non-white the remainder of the task he formerly carried out".[10] He repeated the promise made by the industry that no single white man would lose his job should the gates be opened to the masses of non-whites now clamouring for jobs. He expressed the fear that the inflationary state of South Africa's mining industry, caused principally by "job reservation", might act as a brake on new mining development. It should be noted that Dr. Maltitz was not suggesting equal pay for the blacks or even a narrowing of the wage difference. He was aiming to keep down costs by promoting whites and giving their former jobs to blacks at less pay.

However, Harry Oppenheimer, Chairman of Anglo-American Corporation (the largest mining company in South Africa), has gone even further. He told a meeting of all-white trade unionists in 1971 that prosperity was indivisible and that Africans should therefore receive equal pay for equal work in South Africa.[11] He said this in spite of a warning from Carel de Wet, the Minister of Mines and Planning, that he should cease promoting integration.

Throughout this debate on mining wages, RTZ has stayed silent. It is not known whether the earnings of black miners at Palabora exceed the low levels often enforced by the jealousy of the white trade unions, though RTZ claims that unlike many other mining companies, it allows black miners to bring their families with them. The silence of RTZ contrasts with the outspoken attitude of Oppenheimer and other industrialists who are threatening to subvert the apartheid system. At least three foreign companies have already introduced equal pay for blacks, partly in deference to complaints from the anti-apartheid movement. The first of these was the [American] Polaroid Corporation, which sent an investigation committee, including blacks, to study labour conditions in South Africa. As a result of these recommendations, the company increased the pay of black employees in its South African subsidiary.

In August 1971, South Africa's two biggest banks, the British-owned Barclays and Standard, became the first large-scale employers to introduce equal pay for non-whites. About three hundred African coloured and Asian tellers and clerks were awarded equal pay with their white colleagues. Although the increases were small, since the differences were anyway narrow, the move was a victory for the British anti-apartheid movement, which had long campaigned against these two banks.

So much for the claim that foreign investment automatically means more pay for the Africans. I hope to have shown that most black workers, particularly in the mining industry, are in fact exploited. On the other hand, foreign companies can introduce better pay or even equal pay, if they so wish. I shall now turn to the argument that economic links will mean political progress for the Africans.

One thing should be clear from the start: British business companies deal with South Africa to make money. Even those who claim most fervently that they wish to advance the blacks do not pretend that this was their primary motive for investing in South Africa. The putative benefits of the economic links have never been claimed as more than a side-effect or bonus, additional to commercial gain. Both private companies and British Governments have for years known the excellent quick returns on investments in South Africa. For example, on 4 April 1968 a Labour President of the Board of Trade wrote to John Davies (Director-General of the Confederation of British Industries and later Minister of Technology):

> In 1967 we sent goods worth nearly £260 million to South Africa, or 5 percent of our total exports. South Africa is now one of our biggest markets after the US. Our investment in South Africa has been estimated to be of the order of £1000 million by the Reserve Bank of South Africa; we estimate that about one tenth of UK overseas direct investment is in South Africa. We are also very conscious of the importance attached by South Africa to her exports to the UK: these continue to represent about one third of South Africa's total exports. We have firmly resisted political pressures to terminate the preferential access enjoyed by South African products . . . . Industries here are for their part rightly determined that political differences should not affect their determination to cultivate the opportunities the South African market should continue to offer and I am sure that it is in the interest of all in both countries that such differences should not be allowed to affect the expansion of future trade.[12]

That was written by Labour Cabinet Minister Anthony Crosland. Under his auspices, the Board of Trade did everything possible to increase trade with South Africa. In spite of the fact that South Africa had been expelled from the Commonwealth, two-fifths of her goods coming to Britain paid 10 percent less duty than non-Commonwealth goods. Britain supported South Africa's contravention of GATT (the General Agreement on Tariffs and Trade) even though South Africa's high tariffs hurt Britain. Between 1965 and 1969, Britain's balance of trade with South Africa moved from an £84 million surplus to a £9 million deficit.[13]

Both British business and Governments stand to gain from trade with South Africa. Commercial companies want big dividends: Governments, whether Labour or Tory, want to improve the country's balance of payments. Granted this economic motive, one should be cautious about the subsequent rationalization that British investment will benefit black South Africans. Particularly one should be cautious because the two main theses used to support this argument are mutually contradictory.

The first, or reformist, thesis states, that with the increased prosperity of South Africa, the *apartheid* system will naturally fall away. The non-whites will demand more money in order to buy things like cars, TV sets and washing machines. The manufacturers will support this demand in order to win a new market. Proponents of this thesis make an analogy between the blacks in South Africa today and the British working classes over the last two centuries, who instead of being forced into a revolution, as Marx predicted, are now often house-owners, car-owners, shareholders and therefore well disposed to the capitalist system. The thesis is favoured by British businessmen with South African interests. Sir Val Duncan, for instance, talks of building a "black middle class".

The variant "revolutionary" thesis has been advanced by the *Economist*. According to this, economic advance will make the blacks more aware of political injustice and more prone to revolt. Analogies are made between South Africa in the near future and France in 1789, or Russia in 1917. Both revolutions took place, so it is argued, because of an economic "take-off".

Apart from being mutually contradictory, both theses are full of flaws. Both presuppose that the black population will automatically share in economic improvement. The evidence of the last ten years suggests that they are actually becoming worse off, not just relative to the whites but in absolute terms. Increased wages for blacks have lagged behind the inflation in prices. The mass expulsion of Africans and their resettlement in "Bantustans" has created rural unemployment, homelessness and starvation. The protein deficiency disease "kwashiorkor", which killed at least a million Biafrans during the recent war, is widespread in South Africa. The "reformist" analogy with the British working class ignores the important fact that the South African proletariat are a different race, whom the whites, or ruling class, are used to regard as helots. The "revolutionary" thesis fails to explain why the revolution has not already taken place, since the last ten years have seen the greatest economic "take-off" in South African history, and ignores the overwhelming military superiority of the white regime.

Wishful thinking, sometimes a cover for business interests, ignores the hardening of the apartheid system. In the last few years, South Africa, backed by British investment, has not only consolidated its own domestic tyranny but is spreading its influence and ideas throughout black Africa. South African capital is behind the Cabora Bassa dam in Mozambique, the largest hydroelectric scheme in Africa. South Africa has supported the Smith regime in Rhodesia. More important still, she has extended trade and diplomatic influence to many independent black states such as Malawi, Gabon, Ghana and Ivory Coast. President Nyerere of Tanzania, who had South Africa kicked out of the Commonwealth in 1961, is today one of the few African leaders who remains firmly opposed to a "dialogue" with the *apartheid* states.

This political "dialogue", and the opening up of the continent to commerce with South Africa, is one of her chief attractions for investors from Great Britain. In the succeeding chapters we shall examine how RTZ has spread out from its base in Johannesburg to three neighbouring territories in South Africa's sphere of influence.

NOTES

1. Institute of Directors pamphlet, 8–7–69.
2. *The Times*, 21–9–70.
3. *Financial Times*, 20–5–71.
4. *Daily Telegraph*, 20–5–71.
5. XRAY, August 1971.
6. XRAY, August 1971.
7. *Financial Mail* (Johannesburg), 26–3–70.
8. *South Africa* by Helen Lewis-Jones, p. 5. I am greatly indebted to this excellent booklet for many facts and ideas in this chapter.
9. World Bank figures, 1971.
10. *Australian Financial Review*, 26–6–71.
11. *The Times*, 16–9–71.
12. Letter sent 4–4–68. Quoted in Lewis-Jones.
13. *Private Eye*, 31–7–70.

2. RHODESIA

It will be an ill day for the native races when their fortunes are removed from the impartial and august administration of the Crown and abandoned to the sea of self-interest of a small white population. Such an event is no doubt very remote. Yet the speculator, the planter and the settler are knocking at the door.
——Winston Churchill, then Colonial Secretary, referring to Southern Rhodesia in 1921.

SIR VAL DUNCAN, Chairman of RTZ, declared in 1969:

There was always a fine strain of British thinking which believed that our responsibilities to the countries where we provided Government would not be discharged until we had brought them to self-Government. There was disagreement about timing on this and some voices arguing for a more or less permanent hegemony over some of these countries. But finally, jolted in some cases by the emergent peoples themselves, the concept of self-Government won through, and today we witness the virtual completion of the greatest act of decolonization which has ever been achieved.[1]

But only a "virtual completion". In Southern Rhodesia, a small group of Europeans has broken away from British rule to assert an illegal and tyrannous regime over 5 million black Africans who outnumber them by 20 to 1. The concept of self-Government for the Africans, far from winning through, has been publicly and explicitly flouted by the illegal Prime Minister Ian Smith.

The groups of white men claiming to represent Rhodesia have introduced a regime even worse than South Africa's for the exploitation and brutalizing of Africans. One of their first acts after the declaration of independence in 1965 was to order the hanging of several Africans who had been pardoned by the Crown. Yet white men who kill Africans, in a fit of temper, get three years' prison or less. A white man (with four previous convictions for violence) who flogged and set his dogs on a totally innocent African was sentenced to three months in prison, then promptly released. But an African served three months in prison, including solitary confinement and reduced rations, for having stolen two crates of empty bottles. Scores of thousands of Africans have been turned off their ancestral land to make way for white ranchers. Since UDI the Africans have received progressively less pay, less education, less employment.

The British Government, after renouncing the use of force, could bring pressure to bear on Rhodesia only by economic sanctions.* Although South Africa refused to enforce sanctions against a fellow *apartheid* regime, the measures have hurt Rhodesia ever since UDI. Tobacco growers found it difficult to sell their goods, although they were recompensed by heavy Government subsidies. The transport industries, especially the railways, have been starved of investment. One effect of sanctions has been to prevent the white regime from effecting some of its most cruel *apartheid* policies. As the *Sunday Times* reported on 10 October 1971:

> The Rhodesian Front congress and the municipal council both heard proposals last week for moving the Africans in townships around Salisbury lock-stock-and-barrel into the tribal trust lands, or designated African areas. The proposals were defeated or with-drawn, but they illustrate the dilemma of the Rhodesian Front: the majority of its supporters want a white-dominated society closer to the South African model; but they are even less able than white South Africans to pay for it.[2]

The illegal Rhodesian regime would have been in serious trouble and might have had to capitulate, if it had not been able to exploit and sell its newly discovered minerals. And the company that was foremost in mining and selling these minerals, thus boosting the balance of payments of the illegal Smith regime, was Rio Tinto

---

* This was written after the "settlement" between Britain and Rhodesia but before the official lifting of sanctions, which is anticipated for mid-1972.

(Rhodesia).* The activities of this company are at variance with Sir Val Duncan's "concept of self-Government".

Rio Tinto began to prospect in 1956 near Gatooma in what was then Southern Rhodesia, a part of the Central African Federation. Two Europeans and 300 "boys" worked on what had been named the Empress Nickel Prospect. In April 1957, R. A. Georges, Assistant Chief Mining Engineer to Rio Tinto (Southern Rhodesia) Ltd., told a party of visiting journalists: "If we are able to start up a mine here (as distinct from a mere prospect) then the Federation will become one of the few countries that can include nickel in its list of products for, as you know, 90 percent of the total western world's output of nickel comes from Canada...."[3] In October 1957, however, a report to the shareholders of Rio Tinto had this to say of the Empress Nickel Prospect: "... while progress to date has been satisfactory, the fall in the price of copper and the weakening in the demand for nickel has postponed the date of full-scale development."[4]

In the summer of 1965, during the period of angry arguments that ended with UDI, the world prices of nickel and copper were rising. Perhaps because of this, Rio Tinto erected a pilot plant at the Empress Prospect, and operations commenced on the main shaft. In August 1967, Rio Tinto (Rhodesia) announced that it was going to raise £500,000 on the local market to help finance its programmes at the copper and nickel Empress mine. Since the Empress Mine lies in a tribal trust territory, to which casual visitors can be barred, its activities remained clothed in mystery until May 1969, when some Rhodesian journalists were flown to the mine on a visit that lasted "less than seven hours——to the mine and back". To quote the official *Journal of the Chamber of Mines for Rhodesia* (whose Honorary President is the President of Rhodesia): "Because of the somewhat delicate international situation in which the country finds itself at the present time, what almost amounts to a veil of secrecy has been drawn over what has been taking place." The author lifted the veil to provide some technical information as well as a heartening account of the popularity of the mine: "The impact of a European community on the local tribesmen has been tremendous and the degree of co-

---

* Rio Tinto (Rhodesia) is an offshoot of RTZ, although the RTZ Group no longer includes Rio Tinto (Rhodesia) in its financial accounts.

operation that has been built up between the two peoples, each enjoying their own way of life, stands out as a lesson in race relations." This sanguine report, made after so brief a visit, does not reveal whether Rio Tinto (Rhodesia) was paying a royalty to the tribesmen for operating a mine on their land. However, the *Journal* did reveal the assets of the mine as being "in excess of £4,000,000 . . . and production during 1969 will build up the stockpiles necessary for full production at a later date".[5]

But Rio Tinto (Rhodesia) remained very shy of publicity. In case it should be thought that I exaggerate this secrecy, let me quote once again, this time from an article by "Orebody" in *African Development*, a businessmen's journal, of December 1969. Under a headline "Rhodesia's secret nickel mines", "Orebody" states:

A veil of secrecy hangs over Rhodesian nickel mining, due as much to the concern of the Rhodesian authorities about the revelation of economic secrets as the British Government's determination to penalize sanctions busters. What the Rhodesians are trying to avoid is any move against buyers of their minerals, including nickel, in countries which professedly support sanctions and their efforts in this direction have imposed a curtain on the flow of information about Rhodesia's new nickel. Even Anglo-American Corporation, which with its head office in South Africa would appear to be relatively immune from fears of this nature, is very reluctant to talk about its new mines, while RTZ says in London that it really knows nothing at all about its Empress Mine.[6]

While finding it difficult to believe that the parent group allowed its subsidiary to pursue its own ends without any contact with head office, "Orebody" considered it probable that RTZ exerted no influence on Rio Tinto (Rhodesia).

With or without the advice of its London parent company, Rio Tinto (Rhodesia) had become a thriving concern. In February 1971 it announced that it would shortly open the recently purchased Perseverance Mine near Chakari. With Empress, this would bring Rhodesia's nickel mines up to four; a fifth was announced in September by Johannesburg Consolidated Investment Company. At the same time Rio Tinto announced that it was closing its gold mine at Pickstone from which it would transfer the plant and seventeen Europeans to Perseverance, 48 kilometres away. The statement announced disappointing results from gold and emerald mines but said that the Company had exercised an option on the Tim and Basil gold claims adjacent to the Batchway mines. This would increase the ore reserves and extend the life of the mine. The group had applied for prospecting rights for coal in the Gogwe area, and had been granted prospecting rights in the Lalapanzi area for chrome and in the Hartley area for nickel, copper and platinum.

Rio Tinto (Rhodesia) did not confine itself to mining. Like many Rhodesian companies it has diversified into industry, producing agricultural machinery and irrigation equipment. A British business journal remarked with an air of surprise that this company that had sprang into prominence only a few years ago was "acquiring something of a conglomerate image".[7]

Rio Tinto (Rhodesia) had also grown rich. In 1969, the unaudited profits of this fledgeling company in a smal country harassed by sanctions were R$1,520,000. (The Rhodesian dollar equals the South African Rand.) By the following year its profits had risen to R$2,812,000.[8] Whoever was hurt by sanctions, it was not Rio Tinto (Rhodesia).

The value of Rio Tinto (Rhodesia) to the economy of Rhodesia can be deduced from the statements of the regime's officials. An economic survey published on 27 April 1971 by the Ministry of Finance revealed that economic growth had slowed to 4·6 percent during 1970, compared with almost 10 percent in 1969. The Treasury expected "more vigorous growth" during 1971 but warned that even with increased mining and manufacturing exports, the country's balance of payments would remain under "considerable strain". With agricultural output virtually static, the growth in the economy came from mining (up 12 percent to a record of R$99 million), manufacturing up, 14 percent and construction, up 13 percent. It was pointed out that the 1970 exports and imports, although higher than in any other post-sanctions year, were still below the level of 1965.

It should be remarked that Rhodesia's exports before sanctions were principally in goods like tobacco and asbestos which have been most hit by sanctions. Her economic recovery is due to the growth of manufacture and mining, above all mining, since the ore was easy to sell in contravention of sanctions. This dependence on mining was admitted implicitly by John Wrathall, Rhodesian Minister of Finance, in his budget speech on 15 July 1971. After pointing out the remarkable progress made by the Rhodesian economy in the five and a half years since sanctions had been imposed, Wrathall said there was now a slowing down in some sectors. The tonnage of minerals produced in Rhodesia had increased steadily but base metal prices had weakened and the total value of mineral production in the first five months of that year had fallen 8 percent from the same period in the previous year. The Secretary for Mines, Mr. Parjer, said that only this price drop had prevented the value of mineral production from reaching the R$100 mark, but hoped that the "magical figure" would be attained in 1971. The industry, he revealed, was striving to reach the target of R$200 by the mid-1970s.

How much of the mineral production reached in 1970 is attributable to Rio Tinto (Rhodesia)? It has been suggested that the Empress Mine was producing 6000 tons of nickel a year from 1970. Since the fixed assets of the Empress mine were given in 1969 as about £4 million and the profits of the company as more than £1 million, one can deduce a tidy return on capital invested. One cannot deduce where these minerals were sold. Of the three Rhodesian nickel producers, the other two, Anglo-American and JCI, are based in Johannesburg and enjoy a natural sales outlet in South Africa. One might assume that much of their nickel goes to South Africa's growing steel industry. If on the other hand, the produce of Rio Tinto (Rhodesia) was finding its way to countries, like Germany and Japan, that professed to favour sanctions, the fault could not be held against RTZ, the parent company, which knew "nothing at all about its Empress Mine".

NOTES

1. The Institute of Directors, Lecture, 8–7–69.
2. *Sunday Times*, 10–10–71.
3. Rio Tinto (Southern Rhodesia) Press statement, 16–4–57.
4. *Rand Daily Mail*, 11–10–57.
5. *Chamber of Mines Journal* (Salisbury), May 1969.
6. *Africa Development*, September 1971.
7. *The Director*, September 1971.
8. *Star* (Johannesburg), 12–2–71.

3. LESOTHO

SOME big mining companies, such as RTZ, choose to operate in countries with stable, white and conservative governments. Others are ready to invest in the more volatile states of the "third world", counting on high profits to compensate for possible political trouble. For example, Lonrho, another British mining company, has investments not only in South Africa and Rhodesia, but in Zambia, Congo-Kinshasa, Ghana, Sierra Leone and Sudan. However, there are some nominally independent black African states which have become, by reasons of geography and economics, virtual dependencies of South Africa. One of these is Lesotho, a small mountainous kingdom enclosed on all sides by South Africa, which provides most of its employment, communications and even security. Both RTZ and Lonrho operate in Lesotho. Indeed, they are the main foreign companies in the country.

The Lesotho kingdom dates to the early nineteenth century, when a brave and wise leader. Mosheshoe (*Mo-shesh-we*), rallied his tribe in a mountain fastness against the threat of attack from the Zulus and other enemies. The British from Cape Province tried to subdue Mosheshoe but their lancers were ambushed and savaged while moving through a gorge. Yet Mosheshoe became a Christian and, when his people were threatened by land-hungry Boers from the Orange Free State, he asked the British for help. The Basutoland Protectorate was to become scarcely distinguishable from a British colony; but the Basuto kings and the literate, very political people preferred British rule to the servile status of black men in South Africa. Lesotho is so poor that 90 percent of the adult male population have at one time had to go to work in South Africa, usually in the mines. This experience has produced a general and deep dislike of the *apartheid* system.

As most of Britain's black African colonies were gaining their freedom during the fifties and sixties, many Basutos feared that independence, without economic strength, would put them at the mercy of their white South African neighbour. The British Labour Party, while still in Opposition, pressed the Government to give more aid to Basutoland, Swaziland and Bechuanaland (now Botswana), before pressing them into self-government. The Labour leader, Harold Wilson, said in May 1963 that he was growing "increasingly fearful"[1] about the future of these Protectorates. But once in office, the Labour politicians overcame these fears for the sake of friendship and trade with South Africa. At the start of Basutoland's final constitutional conference in June 1966, the Labour Colonial Secretary, Fred Lee, acknowledged that the strength of opposition to independence might be a bad omen. The *Observer*'s African correspondent, Colin Legum, questioned the wisdom of giving independence to Basutoland under a "minority and unrepresentative Government". He called this decision "the most dishonest transaction in the recent history of the handover of British power in her colonies".[2]

A month later, Legum grew even more vehement about Britain's policy to the three protectorates:

> What is in fact happening is that we are abandoning [the territories] without any of the defences they need to stay independent of Dr. Verwoerd's Republic. The policy of Mr. Wilson's Government was initiated by the Tories in 1963. It was then, as can now be seen so clearly in retrospect, that Britain decided to pull out of Southern Africa. Partly it was feared that the alternative policy of propping up the Protectorates would become increasingly messy and expensive: partly it was felt that such a course would lead to increasingly strained relations with Dr. Verwoerd and might ultimately involve us in a direct confrontation with him.[3]

The more conservative *Sunday Times* declared: "The British Government, seemingly intent on getting out of Basutoland as cheaply as possible, has refused to put up the money, or even promise grants-in-aid to balance the budget. The combination of the Colonial Office's skilful lack of commitment to Basutoland and Dr. Verwoerd's canny waiting game seems likely to squeeze [the Basuto Premier] into a completely subservient policy of "neighbourliness'."[4]

When Lesotho became independent a few weeks later, its Prime Minister, Chief Leabua Jonathan, was obliged to rely for support on Britain and South Africa. As a descendant of the great King Mosheshoe and an experienced politician, Chief Jonathan had won the general election held in 1965, one year before independence. His rival was Ntsu Mokhehle, whose party had an affinity with the banned Pan African Congress of South Africa. Although Mokhehle and his supporters stood to the left of Chief Jonathan, they knew that outright hostility to South Africa was made impossible by economic factors.

Lesotho's main source of revenue is the remittances home from workers in South Africa. In 1970 this amounted to £4,500,000——nearly ten times the amount of the major export, wool. However, many thousands of Lesothos try their luck searching for diamonds on or near the surface of the remote north-east of the country. Their finds of sometimes colossal stones have encouraged foreign companies to prospect with a view to large-scale industrial mining. The South African De Beers group were among those who gave up——discouraged as much by the bad mountain roads as by the lack of diamonds. However, in October 1967, Chief Jonathan and Val Duncan, Chairman of RTZ, announced an agreement in principle on a prospecting and operating programme for the Lesotho State diamond deposit at Letseng-la-Terai, which lies at an altitude of 10,000 feet in the Mokhotlong district of north-east Lesotho. Small scale workings on this deposit had already produced diamonds to a value of R2 million. The formal agreement would be for a minimum of 25 years, including a two-year prospecting period during which Rio Tinto's expenditure would be at the rate of R250,000 a year. According to the *Rand Daily Mail*, the company had programmed for an expenditure of R6 million.[5] It was pointed out with relief in Johannesburg financial circles that since Charter Consolidated had a stake in RTZ, this British company would be bound to stick to the marketing arrangements of the diamond Central Selling Organization.

The future of RTZ in Lesotho is closely linked with that of Chief Jonathan, who signed the initial agreement. Then the legal Prime Minister, Chief Jonathan has since mounted a coup d'état, suspended the constitution, and made himself a dictator. The turn of events occurred during the general election of January 1970. For months before the election, Chief Jonathan had dropped hints that he favoured a one-party state. His own party, the BNP, had won in 1965 by only six votes over Mokhehle's BCP. Moreover, the Communists and the King's party had since taken the opposition side, leaving Chief Jonathan with a majority of only two votes. As the election campaign warmed up, Mokhehle sounded increasingly radical. On 26 January he told a news conference that he planned to "develop co-operatives in a Socialist society because, in under-developed countries, there is no room for capitalism". Denying "communist leanings", Mokhehle said that he would not nationalize local businesses but wanted them "locally managed on the principle that if they have no faith in the black man they have no right to be here".[6]

Polling began on 27 January when the Lesotho information department reported that all was quiet. However, it soon became clear from returns that the opposition BCP was forging ahead of Chief Jonathan's BNP. Reports came that a man had been shot when riot police opened fire on a crowd in northern Lesotho. The Government Radio, which had first described the polling as peaceful, now told of widespread violence and intimidation by the opposition BCP. At 9.30 p.m. on 29 January, the BCP were reportedly one seat ahead of Chief Jonathan's BNP, who were also accused of holding back unfavourable results. On the morning of 30 January, Mokhehle claimed to have won 33 of the 60 seats against 23 for the BNP. At three in the afternoon on the same day, Chief Jonathan went on the air to declare a state of emergency and the suspension of the constitution. He claimed that: "An atmosphere and threats of violence was spread throughout the country by the opposition on the eve of the election. On the election day, the elections were marred by actual acts of violence all over the country. Now that I have declared a state of emergency, I hereby suspend the constitution, pending the drafting of a new one."[7]

Half an hour after this broadcast, Mokhehle was taken to prison, where he persisted in claiming a victory at the polls. The following day, 31 January, King Mosheshoe II was also arrested. Many hundreds of opposition supporters were questioned and later detained by the police.

In the days after the coup d'état, many white people left the country. It was suggested in Lesotho and by newspapers in black

African states that South Africa had encouraged Chief Jonathan to defy the results of the election. I gather that this was not the case.[8] The South African Ministry of Foreign Affairs is subtle in its approach to independent black states and fears being suspected of interference. Moreover, it would prefer to deal with a left-wing popular government, such as Mokhehle's, rather than with a rump regime like Chief Jonathan's; and the Afrikaners are sticklers for legality and disapprove of revolutions. Immediately after the coup, the South Africans withdrew their advisers, including the Chief Justice, with the result that the opposition leaders could not appeal to the courts. The British advisers stayed, as did F. J. Roach, the British Commissioner of Police. In his support of Chief Jonathan, Mr. Roach was inspired by ideological fervour. In a speech in 1971, given at Bloemfontein, South Africa, Roach appealed for help to his employer Chief Jonathan: "He hates communism and is fighting it." He went on to say that the overthrow of the free world had been planned in Shanghai in 1926 by the then Comintern. "Arrows were drawn on the map of the world and one of the biggest pointed to Africa——right in the middle of the continent. Countries such as Tanganyika, Zanzibar, the Sudan, Somalia and the Congo have all since become communist-dominated," Roach revealed. "Other arrows on that map point towards South Africa and Rhodesia. Communists are clever people. They seek to conquer through infiltration into education, the civil service, political parties, trade unions and churches."[9]

Although Roach had been recruited by Britain's Ministry of Overseas Development, the Minister, Mrs. Judith Hart, did not give him moral support. She told the Commons on 19 February 1970 that the UK had suspended aid to Lesotho "until the position is clarified". The indignant Chief Jonathan replied that the British Government ". . . is recklessly prepared to endanger the lives of one million people in its attempt to use Lesotho as a pawn to restrict South African influence in Southern Africa. If Mr. Wilson thinks he will in this way force me to surrender my country to the Communist-backed opposition parties which he would like to see in power, he is making a serious mistake."[10]

During the months after the coup d'état, there were several violent encounters between Roach's Mobile Police Unit and followers of the imprisoned Mokhehle. Discontent was extreme among the miners of eastern Lesotho. Police headquarters announced in Maseru on 7 April 1970 that at least 20 members of an armed gang had been killed by the police in the Eastern Mokhotlong District. The police claimed to have opened fire on the gang when it shot dead a white South African during a raid on a diamond mine. Police Headquarters further revealed that "an unspecified number of people were killed when a strong combined force of para-military police from the mobile unit and police regulars took control of Kao in the Eastern Mountain Region".[11] A Rhodesian technician who had been held as hostage at Kao claimed that 150 people were killed there during the first week of April. The magazine *Africa* has printed a story confirming what I was told on good authority in Maseru——that the Mobile Police Unit used a light aircraft to drop hand-grenades on Chief Jonathan's opponents, who were almost all diamond miners.[12] Most accounts agree that from March to September 1970, at least 300 people were killed in north-east Lesotho.

After the coup d'état, Chief Jonathan promised Lesotho a five-year "holiday" from politics. But hostility to the regime is widespread, particularly among the diamond diggers of the north-east. A bitter enemy of Chief Jonathan told me that he was one of the 400 civil servants dismissed after the coup, of whom 200 were still in prison. What angered him most was that many Lesotho officials, typists, and clerks had been replaced by British people, at three times the pay for the same job. The proliferation of white people in business, administration, and the professions is remarkable for an African country. It is all the more reprehensible since Lesotho enjoys an 85 percent literacy rate and could fill most of these jobs from the local unemployed. But Chief Jonathan, knowing he cannot trust in the loyalty of his own Lesotho people, prefers to employ expatriates, such as the Chief of Police.

In his relations with South Africa, Chief Jonathan is polite but by no means servile. He was one of the few Commonwealth Premiers who did not object to Britain's sending arms to South Africa. The question, he stated ponderously, should be "viewed in global perspective and not in isolation".[13] He claims to have coined the word "dialogue" for an understanding between South Africa and black African states, while he and his representatives have frequently been to South Africa. "Do you think that I enjoy dining with blacks?"

asked Hendrik Schoeman, a South African cabinet minister, after receiving two Lesothans. "But I had to do it as it was beneficial to my country."[14] However, Chief Jonathan does not conceal his dislike of the apartheid system. When he warned in October 1971 that there could be no stability in southern Africa without majority rule, the South African Premier, Dr. Vorster, was stung into a peevish reply: "I wish in all friendliness to say to him (Chief Jonathan) that there are many things in Lesotho about which I can express myself, but for reasons of friendship I refrain from doing. He must, however, not tempt me too far."[15]

In Lesotho's capital of Maseru, the lack of a colour bar is bewildering, sometimes shocking, for visitors from South Africa, half a mile away. On my first evening at the Lancers Inn, I opened the door of the bar, saw an African drinking, and backed away, as though I had blundered into a ladies' lavatory. After only a few weeks in South Africa, I had once again grown conditioned to the complete social *apartheid*. In Lesotho, white visitors from South Africa have to accept integration. For some, the liberals, this brings a sense of emancipation. A white engineer from Johannesburg, whom I met in Maseru's lively discotheque, said that he had to come to Maseru every few months or burst with rage at *apartheid*. For most white South Africans, talking to blacks is a rare and illuminating experience. By coming to Lesotho, they can find out what the blacks in South Africa are thinking. Moreover, only a very crass visitor could not be impressed by the courtesy and intelligence of the Lesotho people, a proud and delightful race. An Afrikaner official attached to the Government in Lesotho said that both sides benefited from mixing: "The Lesotho all know what we're like in South Africa. But here I think they see another side of us. . . . They are really very nice people. So polite. If *you* bang your head getting out of your car, *they* say 'I'm sorry'."

The Lesotho look on the visitors from South Africa with rather quizzical interest. One man said of the tourists: "They are mostly Boer farmers from the Orange Free State——great burly Calvinists who wouldn't even discuss the state of the crops with one of their African farm-hands. But when they come over here they are very anxious to meet an African girl. The Basuto girls are very well behaved. She might show a bit of thigh and offer to show you round

Maseru, and afterwards you might find yourself in her room in
Maseru township. But it's not like Swaziland. There, so I've heard,
the girls stop the white drivers in the road and ask how much they
want for a round or for the night. They make love in the grounds of
the hotel." Such behaviour would not take place at the Lancers Inn,
where the Lesotho maid, after cleaning my room, would prop up the
Gideon Bible opened at a text she thought suitable——usually Job or
Isaiah.

The economic damage done by the coup d'état has made Lesotho
still more dependent on outside help. In 1969, the year before the
coup, the value of diamond exports from Lesotho reached a record
R1,173,502——about 15 percent above the previous record of
1967.[16] These diamonds were produced almost entirely by small
companies or individual diggers. During the first four months of
1970, when unrest was sweeping north-east Lesotho, the production
of diamonds was worth only R122,393——one quarter the total for
the corresponding four months of 1969.[17] To recompense for this
loss, Lesotho allowed a foreign company to build an £800,000 hotel
complex for South African tourists.[18] The hotel casino is one of the
strangest spectacles in Africa. Beefy Boer farmers, black Lesotho
officials and West Europeans from the United Nations can be seen
seated together round the roulette wheel, whose croupier, a Bavarian
girl, takes a tidy income in tips: "For ze personnel. Zenk you,
messieurs!" One of the leading gamblers is a copper-coloured Lesotho, dressed like a "gaylord" on a Mississipi steamer, in frilled shirt,
maroon bow tie, and purple dinner jacket and trousers. There are so
many fruit-machines that the responsible engineer, an Englishman,
told me it took him from eight in the morning till two at night to
keep them in working order. He advised me: "You have a far better
chance of winning on the 50c machines, which are American, than on
the 20c machines, which are Australian. When it comes to fruit machine electronics, the Americans are ten years behind the Australians."

Although the Lesotho Government takes a percentage of the
profits of the hotel and the casino, the tourist industry has its disadvantages. Since most of the tourists come from South Africa, Lesotho dares not take any political action that might offend its
visitors. The conspicuous opulence of the Holiday Inn and of its

almost exclusively white guests is a cause of bitterness to the poorer Lesothos. Unlike such countries as Yugoslavia and Germany, Lesotho has not brought in a law forbidding its own nationals to gamble at the casino. Officials in all poor African countries are susceptible to corruption, but temptation must be worse in Lesotho, where civil servants are seen every evening wasting their salaries at the gaming table. Lesotho, like Swaziland (another former protectorate), has become for southern Africa what Tangiers once was in the north. It thrives on the puritanism that is enforced by law in South Africa, where gambling is illegal, the pubs and cinemas are shut on Sundays,* and sexual intercourse is forbidden with people of another race. Lesotho is being prostituted by poverty.

Many Lesothos hope that the economy can be saved by large-scale diamond mining. The United Nations Development Programme allocated $500,000 in 1971 to exploit diamond-bearing kimberlite, Lesotho's only known mineral resource. The Maluti Diamond Corporation, jointly owned by Lonrho and America's Newmont Mining, obtained prospecting rights, later that year, to work in the Maluti mountains. But an RTZ official with whom I spoke in Maseru suggested that his company had not made great progress so far: "The results have not been as encouraging as they might have been, but if there is a possibility of going ahead we'd be very glad because we'd really like to help this country."

RTZ has so far been little help to Lesotho. During a period of prospecting the host country expects economic benefits from the provision of food supplies and from construction work. But RTZ's supply camp and offices for the Lesotho mine are at Ficksburg, one mile over the border in South Africa. According to RTZ, Ficksburg was chosen because it was convenient for construction work and for getting food supplies that were not available in Maseru. But a suitable site on Lesotho territory was available at Ficksburg Bridge, which is linked by a railway line with Ficksburg over the border. Moreover, Ficksburg Bridge has been developed by the Lesotho Government as a light industrial centre and therefore presumably has facilities for construction work.

An official of the Lesotho Ministry of Mines said he was worried to

* In the neighbouring Orange Free State, even fishing is forbidden on Sundays.

hear that RTZ had taken an option for still more land at Ficksburg: "I think we may take that up with them if the contract comes up for renewal. Maybe the taxes are lower there [in South Africa]. Or maybe it's because there's less danger of looting at Ficksburg. They may be thinking of what happened last May."[19] He was referring to the uprising against Chief Jonathan by miners in north-east Lesotho.

NOTES

1. *Labour's Record on Southern Africa*, by Anne Darnborough, p. 5.
2. *Observer*, 19–6–66.
3. *Observer*, 17–7–66.
4. *Sunday Times*, 12–6–66.
5. *Rand Daily Mail*, 25–10–67.
6. *Africa Research Bureau.* Quoting agencies.
7. *Times*, 31–1–70.
8. From conversation in Maseru. Attribution of remarks is impossible since Lesotho is a police state.
9. *Rand Daily Mail*, April 1971.
10. *The Times*, 23–2–71.
11. *East African Standard*, 8–4–71.
12. *Africa*, No. 3, 1971.
13. *Radio Johannesburg*, 25–2–71.
14. *Times*, 24–11–70.
15. *Times*, 6–10–71.
16. *Financial Gazette* (Johannesburg), n.d.
17. *Financial Gazette*, 3–7–70.
18. *Africa*, No. 3, 1971.
19. Interview with author. April 1971.

4. SOUTH WEST AFRICA

The mandatory state should look upon its position as a great trust and honour, not as an office of profit or a position of private advantage for it or its nationals.
——General Smuts in *League of Nations: A practical System*. Published in 1918.

The South West African case arouses passions not only because an international trust has been betrayed, but also because South Africa herself is the delinquent nation of the world. . . . It is bad enough that a mandate is withheld from international supervision and a dependent people blocked from development to independence under the tutelage of a world body. It is a thousand times worse that the country which has betrayed the trust should have become a by-word in the twentieth century for obscurantist racial philosophies and fierce discrimination against peoples on the grounds of their colour.
——Ruth First in *South West Africa*. Published in 1963.

RTZ's opening of a uranium mine in South West Africa was a major political triumph for South Africa's *apartheid* regime. The news broke in 1969, when the United Nations had already declared that South Africa's occupancy of this territory was illegal. Since then the International Court of Justice at the Hague has declared, in an advisory ruling, that South Africa is under obligation to withdraw its administration from the territory and to cease the occupation which began when the former German colony became a League of Nations mandate after the First World War. The news that a big British company (RTZ) was mining uranium in South West Africa suggested that Britain had defied the United Nations and later the International

Court. The suggestion became a certainty when it was learned, in August 1970, that Britain's Atomic Energy Authority, with the approval of the Labour Government, had signed a contract with RTZ to buy uranium from the South West African mine. The implications of this were so sensational that RTZ made the front page lead article of the London *Observer*.

The search for minerals and above all for copper brought Europeans to South West Africa in the 1850s. The country's coast had been visited as early as 1484, when the Portuguese erected a cross on a stone crag near Swakopmund——not far from the RTZ mine. But the fertile and mineral-rich interior of the country is barred from the sea by the sand dunes and salt flats of the Namib desert. The Skeleton Coast, as it is still called by sailors, is chilled by currents from the Antarctic and blanketed in the morning by a disagreeable drizzle. In 1854, an English Jew, Aaron de Pass, set up coastal trading posts from which he shipped bird guano and salted fish, as well as minerals bartered from the natives of the interior. De Pass later travelled by ox-wagon across the Namib desert to the interior plateau, which lies at about 5000 feet. He and other traders established peaceful relations with tribes such as the Namas and the Hereros. German missionaries had already begun to preach in this region, where they were also active as traders. Although the Africans were reluctant converts, they patronized the missionary stores, and Herero women still wear the Mother Hubbard dresses that were thought respectable by the missionaries' wives. "The missionary and the trader must precede the soldier," said Bismarck, and in the 1880s German troops arrived at Swakopmund. A sphere of influence was marked out, roughly equivalent to the present South West Africa, while the German commanders strengthened their power by treaties with the tribes. The Hereros and the Namas, who had long been rivals for pastureland and cattle, were encouraged by the Germans to engage in serious war. When the Germans at one point sided with the Hereros, the Nama Chief, Hendrik Witbooi, wrote to his hereditary enemy, Maharero, a sad and prophetic letter:

You are to be protected and helped by the German Government but, my dear Captain, do you appreciate what you have done? Do you imagine you will retain all the rights of your independent chieftainship after you shall have destroyed me (if you succeed)? You will have bitter eternal remorse for this handing of your land and sovereignty over to the hands of White people. This giving of yourself into the hands of the Whites will become to you a burden as if you were carrying the sun on your back.[1]

The most famous governor of the colony, Theodor Leutwein, later wrote that he had used his

> best endeavour to make the native tribes serve our cause and to play them off one against the other. Even an adversary of this policy must concede to me that it was more difficult but also more serviceable to influence the natives to kill each other than for us to expect streams of blood and streams of money from the Old Fatherland for their suppression.[2]

In the light of these sentiments it is surprising to learn that Leutwein was looked upon by most of the German settlers as too patient and too kind to the Africans. In particular he was accused of being lenient with the Hereros living close to the main German settlements at Windhoek and Okahandja. Although Leutwein had pushed the Hereros out of ancestral land, and had confiscated thousands of cattle as fines for alleged breaches of treaty, he yet insisted on treating them as people with rights and a measure of dignity. When a Windhoek baker struck a Herero dignitary and threw him out of the shop, Leutwein castigated the German for ill-treating "a proud and respected man and a particularly wealthy cattle-owner".[3] At a meeting of Germans at Windhoek in 1896, speakers argued that Leutwein went too far in recognizing the interests of the tribes and the chiefs. They called his policy too wild, in particular during times of unrest and during disputes over boundaries. One delegate from the nearby township of Klein-Windhoek claimed to represent the majority of the settlers when he called for war against the Hereros to obtain "a military solution of this problem".[4] Although this view was voted down at the time, German opinion grew increasingly hostile to the Hereros. On the eve of the Herero war in January 1904, the *Deutsche Südwestafrikanische Zeitung* carried a letter that spoke for the German majority in attacking "friends of the mission", the "idealists" and the "wishy-washy humanitarianism" of the Government.[5]

The Hereros, long threatened and deeply provoked, struck the first blow against their oppressors. In the second week of January 1904, they killed more than a hundred German men, soldiers and settlers, and blew up the railway line between Windhoek and Swakopmund. Although the Hereros had spared the lives of women and children as well as of German men whose behaviour had been decent, the Germans replied with a sadistic ferocity that is still remembered as infamous in this century of atrocities. When the Herero people were beaten in battle and fleeing with their families to the east, the German General von Trotha threw a cordon to seal off their escape routes and then issued his *Vernichtungs Befehl*, or extermination order. A German soldier who served in the campaign described how *Vernichtungs Befehl* had operated when his unit caught up with the fleeing Hereros: "We led the men away to one side and shot them. The women and children, who looked pitiably starved, we hunted into the bush." He later described what became of these fugitives:

A number of babies lay helplessly languishing by mothers whose breasts hung down long and flabby. Others were lying alone still living, with eyes and nose full of flies. Somebody sent out our black drivers and I think they helped them to die. All this life lay scattered there, both man and beast, broken in the knees, helpless still in agony, or already motionless, it looked as if it had all been thrown out of the air. In the last frenzy of despair man and beast will plunge wildly into the bush somewhere, anywhere, to find water, and in the bush they will die of thirst.[6]

The *Vernichtungs Befehl* was not obeyed to the letter. Out of 80,000 Hereros before the war, about 15,000 escaped to the Kalahari desert.

Later that year, the German army dealt with the tribes in the south. Chief Hendrik Witbooi, whose warning to the Hereros had been so foolishly ignored, was now 80 years old but still fit to lead the Namas in battle. When he was killed in action, his followers buried Witbooi and covered the grave with stones so that the body should not fall into the hands of the Germans. Even Leutwein called Witbooi "a born leader and ruler ... who might have become world famous had it not been his fate to be born to a small African tribe".[7]

The Germans had now conquered and crushed the tribes in most of
South West Africa. The exception were the Ovambos, who lived in
the north of the territory next to Portuguese Angola. The Ovambos in
South West Africa alone were as numerous as the southern tribes,
who amounted to only 200,000 people even before the massacres by
the Germans. Since Ovambo land was not attractive to European
farmers and since the German army baulked at another campaign,
the colonial government decided to seal off this northern region and
leave the Ovambos to their own devices. From the Herero war in
1904 to the World War ten years later, the Germans in South West
Africa put their minds to making money. The copper deposits at
Tsumeb were worked by a mining company that also financed a railway to Swakopmund. Diamonds were discovered at Luderitz and
later in many places along the "Skeleton Coast". The colony was
beginning to pay its way when the war broke out in 1914. The Afrikaner generals Botha and Smuts, who had fought so bravely
against the British during the Boer War, now led an army for Britain
against the German colony. The Africans did not take part in this
"white man's war", but were pleased by the German defeat after a
brief campaign. They were soon to find the South Africans just as
unpleasant rulers.

Until late in the war the Allies did not intend to strip Germany of
her colonies. It was General Smuts in 1917 who started to urge the
dismantlement of the enemy's empire. After the war, in the bitter
atmosphere that prevailed at Versailles, the Allies agreed to place
Germany's colony under the care of the newly formed League of
Nations. German East Africa was mandated to Britain, which took
Tanganyika, and Belgium, which took Ruanda-Urundi; the Cam-
eroons and Togoland were each divided between Britain and France;
South West Africa went to South Africa; the small Pacific islands
went to New Zealand and Japan, and German New Guinea to Aus-
tralia, which, as will be seen (in Part II, Chapter 4), has permitted
RTZ to mine on the island of Bougainville.

South Africans like Botha and Smuts were more decent and less
fanatical men than today's Nationalist leaders. But though loyal to
Britain and advocates of democracy, they were nevertheless Boers,
with an almost instinctive disregard for the rights of the black Africans. During the twenty years of the League of Nations mandate, the

South Africans continued and even stepped up the process of white exploitation. After the war, about half the German settlers were permitted to stay, while even those who had been repatriated were soon allowed to return. The land that had belonged to the German Government or concessionary companies was offered cheap to white South Africans who swarmed into the territory that Smuts was claiming to govern as a "sacred trust". The European population trebled to 31,000 under the League of Nations mandate, and the bewildered Africans were pushed into arid reserves without sufficient water or pasture for their flocks. Taxes and fines were imposed to force them to work as cheap labourers on the white men's farms. When the Bondels people refused to pay their dog-tax, the Government sent planes to bomb their village and soldiers to shoot the survivors. One hundred men, women and children were killed out of this small community. The South Africans joined with the Portuguese to suppress malcontents among the Ovambo people, more than a hundred of whom were mown down by South African Maxim guns.

Complaints were made at the League of Nations and quite ignored by the South Africans. During the 1930s, most of the Germans in South West Africa joined the Nazi Party and looked forward to rejoining the Reich. When the American writer Negley Farson stayed at Swakopmund in 1938, the local people boycotted the hotel dance because non-Aryans were in the orchestra. A fearsome old battle-axe, Margareth von Eckenbrecher, who had written a best-selling book in 1902 encouraging settler women to be "brave, strong and happy pioneers", declared in 1937 that the abandoned people of South West Africa stood "true to their homeland, true to the Reich and its Fuehrer, proud to declare themselves German pioneers". Her Aryan rhetoric was interspersed with whining complaints about the ill-treatment of Germans in South West Africa during the First World War. She alleged that their correspondence with Germany had been censored by a Jew who charged them for the delivery of important letters: "He told a certain Dr. F. he had news of his mother. What would he pay? He paid through the nose. The news was of her death."[8] The German Nazis during this period formed close ties of friendship and ideology with extreme Afrikaner Nationalists like Dr. Vorster, the present Premier of South Africa, who was and may still be an admirer of Adolf Hitler.

Since the Nationalists won power in 1952, they have imposed the *apartheid* system on the "mandate" of South West Africa. The encouragement of immigrants, mostly from Germany, means that 17 percent of the population is white. Since most of the blacks are in the Ovambo reserve, the proportion of whites in the rest of the country is higher still. Indeed, Windhoek, the capital, is a largely white town, in contrast to Washington, DC, which is largely black. Whites, though one in seven of the population, have the exclusive use of two-thirds of the land——including the best land. The Africans, landless or overcrowded, lacking capital and agricultural advice, are reduced to working allotments or tending scrawny goats. Much of the labour for the mines and the white farms comes from Ovamboland, whose able-bodied men are dispatched south with labels round their neck giving their names and qualifications. The majority of the government's money for education is spent on white children. There are no facilities for the non-whites to get higher education, and they are discouraged from going to study at "tribal colleges" in South Africa. The first non-white to practise law in the territory was expelled after a two weeks' stay in 1971.

Political feeling in South West Africa appears to divide by racial groups. Most of the 96,000 whites favour the present system, from which they derive economic benefit. Most African tribes——the Hereros, the Namas and the Damaras——are strongly opposed to the Government. The Hereros especially have adopted an attitude of sullen passive resistance to all government measures, even those that are beneficial. When they refused to move out of their old Windhoek township into the new Katutura township, the police opened fire, killing six and wounding 50. That was in 1959, a year before the Sharpeville killings near Johannesburg. The Coloureds, most of them from South Africa, have limited right to complain. The President of their organization said at a speech in Windhoek last year that the Coloureds were still "enslaved" and could not be happy while a married man was not allowed to bring his wife into the territory.

The Africans have no political rights. The leaders of underground movements like SWAPO have been hunted down, tortured, and killed, or sentenced to long terms of imprisonment. The Government can discriminate against rebel tribes like the Hereros by giving the better jobs to Ovambos and other outsiders. The Government encourages and makes much of the ancient tribal disputes between the Hereros, Namas, and Damaras. A champion of South Africa, Patrick Wall, MP, proclaimed last year on the strength of a visit to South West Africa that "the only tribe united in its discontent are the Hereros, who until decimated by the Germans were the master-race and intend to become the dominant faction once again."*⁹

Until this year, defenders of the regime in South West Africa would contrast the truculence of the Hereros with the alleged contentment of the Ovambos, the largest tribe in the territory. Since German times, Ovamboland had been sealed off and allowed to maintain its traditional civilization. Each year an increasingly large number of young Ovambo men were recruited for contract work in the mines outside, even as far as South Africa, but Ovamboland remained separate from the government of the territory. Since whites cannot hold land or do business there, there was no racial conflict. South African propaganda used to boast of Ovamboland as a model of *apartheid*, where blacks were happy living *apart* from the whites. After the World Court decision in 1971, when South Africa was under attack for its South West African policy, some foreign reporters were flown up to Ovamboland on a brief visit. They duly reported idyllic scenes of blacks and whites chatting and playing cards together. They were duly told that the Ovambos did not want independence but were well content with the rule of their chiefs and the friendly help of South Africa. Throughout South West Africa, white people preferred to employ Ovambos as servants and labourers because they were thought to be well behaved. Indeed, some white people have come to use the word "Ovambo" for all blacks regardless of race or language. The myth of the contented Ovambo fell to pieces late in 1971, when 15,000 of them went on strike in protest against low pay rates, the rigid contract system and the law that prevents their bringing families out of Ovamboland. So startled were the South Africans by this movement of defiance that they replied with unusual leniency and conceded some demands. But the Ovambo strike, with its attendant revelations of deep political bitterness, exploded South Africa's last excuse for clinging to South West Africa.

* Since to decimate means to "kill one in ten", Mr. Wall underestimates the *Vernichtungs Befehl*.

There is little internal threat to South Africa's rule over this "mandate", but she has been perturbed at times by the hostility of the United Nations. It was old General Smuts who in 1946 tried to convince the United Nations that South Africa should annex its former mandate. He pointed out the geographical unity of the two territories. He boasted of South Africa's "progressive policy of native administration".[10] He argued that this unity was already a *fait accompli*. He claimed that a referendum had shown an overwhelming majority for annexation by South Africa. The UN delegates doubted whether the population had understood the poll. They felt still more suspicious of South Africa's good intentions when the Nationalist Party, then in Opposition, abused the United Nations. One speaker in South Africa's House of Assembly said that the UN consisted mostly of "Coloured and Asiatic countries, and of countries whose inhabitants are of mixed blood".[11] When the Nationalists came to power, the United Nations grew still more determined not to let the mandate fall into South African hands by law. They were supported in this by the International Court of Justice which affirmed, three times in the 1950s and as many times since, that South West Africa was still a League of Nations mandate. An Anglican priest, Michael Scott, who knew and detested the South West African regime, lent his energy and his eloquence to the cause of its ill-treated subjects.

The debate dragged on into the sixties, when members of the UN South West Africa Committee tried to enter the territory and were threatened by the authorities with arrest. Although British Governments did not join in condemning South Africa at the UN, the British press was occasionally vehement. An editorial in *The Times* in 1960 said of South West Africa:

It was a German possession fiendishly abused. It was placed under the mandate system of the League of Nations in order that its wretched tribesmen might be given a new deal in the light of decent world opinion. Instead of fulfilling this obligation of honour, the South African Government, quibbling barefacedly about the succession from the League of Nations, has swallowed South West Africa into its vile scheme of *apartheid* and has, adding insult to injury, taken advantage of its misdoings to strengthen its parliamentary majority. The Nationalist Party has helped itself to

extra seats out of South West African voters. There is only one
verdict possible in this sorry business. A mandate has been stolen
and the thieves are vainly protesting their innocence.

The views of *The Times* are not shared by Labour or Tory
Governments, which put Britain's commercial interests before the
rights of the South West Africans. When the International Court
ruled in 1971 that South Africa was illegally occupying South West
Africa, the British Government rejected the Court's decision on
legal grounds. Of the fifteen judges on the Court, only the British
and French opposed the decision. Yet the ruling of the Court was a
grave embarrassment to the South African Government. It could
not blame the decision on communism, for even the representative
of South Vietnam had told the Court that South Africa had viol-
ated her mandate by the practice of apartheid. The *Rhodesia Herald*
called the Hague decision a setback to South Africa which would
"make it more difficult for her friends to continue to support her".[12]
It was against this background of international argument that RTZ
opened its mine in South West Africa.

The news of the mine was revealed in dribs and drabs over a
period of two years. A statement from RTZ in London, dated 24
April 1969, quoted Dr. de Wet, South African Minister of Planning:

> A company may be formed to exploit a deposit of uranium in
> the district of Swakopmund, South West Africa, located at Ros-
> sing, which has been under investigation by Rio Tinto South
> Africa for the past two years. . . . If an economic valuation confirms
> the feasibility of a mining operation, a company controlled by the
> Industrial Development Corporation with Rio Tinto as managers
> and secretaries, will be formed.

To which Rio Tinto South Africa added that the RTZ group, besides
being managers of the project would also beneficially hold a majority
of the equity through Rio Tinto South Africa, a wholly owned subsidiary of RTZ.

On 30 January 1970, the UN Security Council recommended
members to avoid economic relations with "Namibia", the name
given to South West Africa by black African nationalists. One month

c

later, the Mining Editor of the *Rand Daily Mail* wrote that Rio Tinto
South Africa was likely to open "the largest mine in Southern Africa"
at Rossing, near Swakopmond. "The uranium ore body," he went on,
"is reported to be about five miles long by one mile wide, of unde-
termined depth."

In June 1970, the Conservatives were returned in the British Gen-
eral Election. A few days later, the new Foreign Minister, Sir Alec
Douglas-Home, stirred a political furore by his announcement that
Britain would sell arms to South Africa. On 5 July a story of over-
whelming importance appeared, tucked away in the *Sunday Times*
Business News. The reporter, Peter Kellner, revealed:

> A secret agreement which will make Britain substantially more
> dependent on South Africa by the mid-1970s for its uranium has
> come to light. Within the past twelve months two contracts have
> been signed between Riofinex, a subsidiary of the mining giant Rio
> Tinto-Zinc, and the UK Atomic Energy Authority to supply Britain
> with 7500 tons of uranium ore between 1973 and 1980 from a new
> mine in South West Africa. But such is the political sensitivity of
> the deal that Harold Wilson issued a directive shortly before the
> election to prevent news of it being made public.

The article went on to reveal that the first deal had been signed in
July 1969. In January 1970 the Ministry informed the Foreign Office
of the agreement, "apparently oblivious of its political implications".
The question had been referred in March 1970 to the Cabinet, which
decided that since the contract had been signed the decision could
not be reversed.

The *Daily Telegraph* soon repeated the gist of the story with the
comment that "the deal means that the Republic has an extra argument in attempts to gain recognition for its disputed South West
Africa guardianship". On 31 July *Private Eye* gave a fuller account of
the deal, and a deeper analysis of its political implications. The
article, based on information from excellent sources, said that the
AEA had approached the Ministry of Technology in 1968 for permission to buy uranium from Rio Algom, a Canadian subsidiary of
RTZ. The contract contained a clause enabling Rio Algom to switch
the contract to Rio Tinto South Africa. The contract, including this
striking clause, was passed by the Minister of Technology, Anthony

Wedgwood Benn. For reasons of its own, RTZ later switched the
contract from Rio Algom to Rio Tinto South Africa, which then began
to negotiate a contract with the South African Industrial Development Corporation, a government body, for the supply of uranium
from Rossing to the AEA and to a German consortium. "This was the
first time South West Africa had been mentioned in any contract,"
wrote *Private Eye*, "and accordingly, AEA again applied to MinTech
for permission to proceed with it. Permission was granted without
reference to Wedgwood Benn." When he heard about it, the new
contract was signed and sealed and the Government took the view
("wrongly" according to *Private Eye*) that the contract could not be
stopped: "The only reaction was a flood of letters from Harold
Wilson to the Ministry of Technology, the Foreign Office and to Rio
Tinto begging for no publicity for the deal before the General Election."

A few days after the *Private Eye* story, the RTZ deal was splashed
on the front page of the *Observer*. "UN defied in uranium deal with S.
Africa" was the headline on the article by Colin Legum. According to
Legum, the plan could count on strong support from John Davies, the
new Minister of Technology, who, as we have seen, favours increased
economic links with South Africa. Moreover Legum pointed out that
uranium supplies from South Africa could be used for Britain's nuclear weapons programme since South Africa did not insist on the
"safety clause" stipulating use for peaceful purposes only.* "But by
committing the Atomic Energy Authority to a long contract," Legum
continued, "the Government may have made Britain's nuclear defence programme partly dependent on South African goodwill."

At this point one should pause to consider the enigmatic role
played in the RTZ uranium deal by Benn, the Minister of Technology.
What can explain his permission for the deal? It cannot be said that
the subject was overlooked among more important matters, since a
contract for uranium is a subject of top priority to the Minister responsible. Nor can Benn be accused of laziness or lack of attention to
detail. The public have seen numerous photographs of him working
away in his office at five o'clock in the morning. A reputed "left
winger", Benn would surely have been suspicious of a uranium deal

---

* Canada insists on the "safety clause". This may be why RTZ had to
switch the AEA contract from Rio Algom to Rio Tinto South Africa.

with South Africa. He defended his decision later by arguing "that the best way of dealing with authoritarian regimes is to increase contacts". But what sort of contact[13] is achieved by buying uranium? Again, did Benn stop to consider what labour conditions prevailed in the mines of Rio Tinto South Africa? Did he not know that its uranium mine was in South West Africa? If so, did he not know that South West Africa was a territory in dispute? Again, did it not occur to Benn, as it occurred to Legum, that uranium from South Africa could have a military as well as a civil purpose? We are told that Benn is an ace technologist. He knows that uranium can be used for the manufacture of nuclear weapons. Did he never stop to consider all, or even one, of these questions?

In 1970, while Britain stood by the South West Africa uranium deal, the United States was discouraging American economic involvement in the territory. The US Government no longer protected American investments made since 1966, when the UN voted to terminate the mandate. On 20 May 1970, the US representative at the UN, Charles Yost, said emphatically that his country would not guarantee investments made by Americans in Namibia.

West Germany, which had wanted to join RTZ in the Rossing venture, was also becoming shy. In October 1970, a spokesman for the Ministry of Education and Science in Bonn confirmed a newspaper report that the Frankfurt Uranium Co. was preparing to join the British company in exploiting the uranium mine. It was understood that the German company would take a 10 per cent share in the venture. However, the West German Government at this time was under attack from black African states for giving credit guarantees to companies helping to build Cabora Bassa dam, in Mozambique, a project that bolstered the economy of this Portuguese colony. The Bonn correspondent of the *Financial Times* said that the Government now had to decide whether to give similar guarantees to the South West African project. He remarked: "News of the Government's dilemma has leaked out only a few days before President Kenneth Kaunda of Zambia and other leaders of the Organization of African Unity are due to make a not entirely welcome visit to Bonn to ask the Government to reverse its Cabora Bassa attitude."[14] In January 1971, the West German Government once more postponed a decision on whether to give credit guarantees to the Frankfurt Uranium Co.

Herr Eppler, the Minister of Economic Co-operation, who is responsible for development aid, said that support for the South West African project would still further damage the country's standing in black Africa. But Government disapproval and cancellation of credit support need not bar a company from investing in South West Africa. American as well as West German firms are active in the territory. Since Yost's statement to the United Nations in May 1970, Gulf Oil, Chevron Oil, Syracuse Oil, and Woodfort Oil and Gas are reported to have taken prospecting concessions.[15] The case of RTZ is unique because the British Government, and a Labour Government at that, not only did not discourage investment but awarded a contract from a state corporation.

Both RTZ and the South African Industrial Development Corporation stand to profit considerably from the Rossing mine on land held in defiance of the International Court. The Africans, the original occupants of this territory, hold no shares and can expect no benefit from the enterprise. Back in 1858, the chiefs of the Nama peoples signed an agreement, ironically called "The League of Nations", by which they pledged themselves to prevent mining in their territory. In September 1971, Chief Kapuuo, the elected head of the Herero people, wrote a letter to his solicitor in London, from which I quote:

> You may well know that apart from its mineral wealth which is substantial, South West Africa is a poor country. The Africans who will be brought to these mines [he lists various mines including Rossing] under the contract labour system, who will work for periods of twelve to eighteen months deprived of their natural family life, unable by current laws to negotiate their salary, and prevented under strict laws from bettering their conditions, benefit but little. This country, which is our country, is being exploited by greedy entrepreneurs, robbed of its wealth, and rendered barren for the future. Our fear is that when freedom finally comes to this land, it will be returned to us with no minerals left. . . . We deplore what the Government in Pretoria is currently allowing. . . . We would like to make it clear that in this matter our appeal as the Herero nation does not in any sense preclude appeals by other African peoples in this territory. At a time when the International

Court has declared South Africa's continuing presence in South West Africa to be illegal, we would urge that immediate steps be taken by the highest bodies to protect the rights of the indigenous peoples of this territory from being exploited. We wish all foreign firms to be removed immediately; we wish to be consulted on ways and means by which our peoples can have a fairer share in benefiting from the wealth of the land of their birth.[16]

Press reports of this letter produced no reply from RTZ. Indeed the company's operations at Rossing are swathed in mystery. RTZ has revealed that the UK Atomic Energy Authority is buying some 7500 tons of uranium, worth £38 million, on a contract running from 1976 to 1982. RTZ has revealed that it will hold a major stake in the mine. RTZ has not disclosed the size of this stake, although it is thought that its share is at least 80 percent. An RTZ spokesman in Johannesburg has revealed an estimate that the mine would employ 700 European miners and 1000 Africans. The rest is virtually silence. Traditionally secretive, RTZ is backed in its Rossing venture by South Africa's Atomic Energy legislation, which makes it an offence to print or utter any unauthorized information about the industry or its products. South African journalists call uranium "the prison mineral". I met with suspicion when I went to South West Africa to ask about the effects of the Rossing mine.

My stay at Windhoek was unproductive. On the first day I met three men——one German, one Canadian, and one Italian——who claimed to have served as mercenaries in the Congo, and one German who claimed to be under sentence of death from the Russians. I spent a Sunday lunch-time at the German club at Okahandja, where some grinning young men, primed with beer and black-currant liqueur, shouted "Heil Hitler!" to see how I responded. Then I took the train to Swakopmund, the summer capital of the territory and the nearest town to the Rossing uranium mine.

Swakopmund lies in the tropics but the cold Antarctic currents give it a climate like summer in the Hebrides. The countryside is a geological freak-show. "Sand-dune researchers" (they actually call themselves that) have come from all over the world to study the local examples, and a Swakopmund man has become an expert "sand-dune skiier". The museum and many bourgeois houses boast specimens of the exotic rocks, crystals and semi-precious stones that are found in this area. You see slabs of aragonite the colour of milky coffee, gargantuan bath salts, pieces of quartz that look like moulding pork or rare beef or tripe. Swakopmund roads are paved with salt that looks like ice and is almost as slippery after rain. The most famous of the flora is *Weltwishia bainesii*, a monstrous tree that sprawls over the ground and lives to be 2000 years old. The sea off Swakopmund is world-famous for anchovies, which bring bigger fish, which in turn bring herds of seals and thousands of stoop-shouldered cormorants.

Swakopmund is a North Sea German resort superimposed on Africa. The neat red-roofed bungalows sport bougainvillea in their gardens. The Gothic gaol (which is still in use), the baroque school, and the Second Reich railway station contrast with the pleasant *jugend-stil* of the private houses. The whaling gun on the sea-front, and the red-and-white striped lighthouse, date to before the First World War, when Swakopmund was famous through southern Africa for its beer-gardens and many cinemas. The native suburb, or *Eingeborenenvorstadt*, is outside Swakopmund, but many African servants are seen carrying white children or taking the dachshunds for a walk. Blacks are permitted to fish but not to swim from the beach; they are employed to carry the fishing rods and to bait the hooks of their white masters.

The opening nearby of the biggest new mine in Africa has had an effect on Swakopmund, but people are frightened to talk of this because of censorship. For example, when Swakopmund and the RTZ mine were front page news in the British press in July and August 1970, the local *Allgemeine Zeitung* reported only the strong views of Swakopmund's Town Clerk concerning the cost of a swimming pool.[17] However, the local press has reported the official statements about the mine made in London and Johannesburg, and it has carried advertisements by RTZ for geologists and field assistants—"Single personnel provided either with free furnished accommodation and boarding at Rossing, or free field living expenses. ... Married personnel provided with unfurnished accommodation at a nominal rental in Swakopmund."[18]

This advertisement explains certain oblique references to RTZ that have been printed in the South West African press. For example, a mining executive, Jim Ratledge, was quoted criticizing "anomalies in the mining law"——by which he meant, though he did not say so, the ban on non-whites in skilled jobs. Reviewing what he called the "worsening white labour position in the territory", Ratledge referred to "a continued inflation of wages or fringe benefits by concerns which must have more labour or close down. . . . As you are well aware, there is hardly a mine in South West Africa which does not build houses for its employees. In the current labour market, to entice a white to a mining camp, it is absolutely essential to provide reasonable housing at a token rental, or free."[19]

The housing boom in Swakopmund, caused by RTZ although the newspapers cannot discuss this, has attracted many Coloureds who are specialists in construction work. This in turn has caused problems, according to P. Ventner, the head of "non-White affairs" in Swakopmund municipality. He told a Town Council meeting in February 1971 that "the poverty among some Coloureds had gone so far that a few had moved into White areas. . . . Part of the Coloured township was busy developing into a shanty town."[20]

I did not find it easy to learn about the mine in conversation. The South African secret police are suspicious of foreign writers; more suspicious of foreign writers who go to South West Africa; most suspicious of foreign writers who go to South West Africa asking for information which is classified as secret under the Atomic Energy Act. However, I was informed by a professional man that the whites employed at Rossing would live at Swakopmund while the blacks, mostly Ovambos, would live by the mine——a site rumoured to be unhealthy owing to radiation. Indeed, the story goes that a geologist first checked the site for uranium when he read that an African chief, in bygone days, had sent his wives to Rossing to make them sterile. A German lawyer told me that the RTZ mine "has meant a great rise in property values, above their real value, but it will be good for the town". A fellow drinker at the bar of the Fuerst Bismarck Hotel on Kaiser Wilhelm Strasse confided to me:

Some people are worried about Swakopmund becoming a mining town instead of a holiday town. It's true that only the married RTZ people will live in Swakopmund while the single men will live in Rossing. But what's to stop them coming here on their nights off? Also I hear that many of these mining people will be from England. . . ."

Here he stopped, recalling that I was a foreigner who spoke bad German.

On my last day in Swakopmund I called at the offices of Rio Tinto Exploration (Pty.) Ltd. and asked for information about the mine. I was advised to telephone "Rossing 1" and to ask for Mr. Fotheringham, Mr. Cook, or Mr. Berning. When I got through, a polite Mr. Fotheringham asked: "Is it an interview you want?" and when I said that it was, he replied that Mr. Berning was out in his car but would ring back. About an hour later, Mr. Cook rang back. "You know our Atomic Energy Act," he said. "I am afraid we cannot give you any information on the site." I asked if he could tell me about the recruitment of personnel or the likely effect of RTZ on the locality. Once again, Mr. Cook politely declined.

A few weeks after my visit to Swakopmund, when I was studying printed material on South Africa's uranium industry, I came to see the reason for the obsessive secrecy. So little is published about uranium in South African newspapers, that the references which are authorized carry added significance. Let us examine some of these statements in their chronological order. On 16 January 1970 Greg Kukard wrote in the *Financial Gazette*:

> The Rossing mine will be Southern Africa's first open-cast uranium mine. Current legislation prohibits the publication of details of South Africa's uranium industry, but it is clear from figures secured by the *Financial Gazette* this week that the proposed mine will produce a very high grade of uranium ore. It is also clear that it will drastically swell South Africa's overall uranium production statistics.

On 2 March 1970 the Mining Editor of the *Rand Daily Mail* wrote:

> The significance of the Rossing project is that its opening will certainly lead to the establishment of a uranium hexafluoride industry in South Africa. Uranium hexafluoride is processed to make enriched fuel for nuclear reactors, but none is made in South Africa

because production is uneconomic below several thousand tons a year.

The article quoted a radio statement by Dr. A. J. A. Roux, the Chairman of the South African Atomic Energy Board, saying that when production of uranium oxide in Southern Africa (N.B. Southern not South) reached 5000 tons a year, uranium hexafluoride production would be economic. Dr. Roux went on:

> Encouraging progress is being made with determining the economic recoverability of the uranium deposit at Rossing. If uranium reclamation at Rossing is realized, South Africa's uranium production potential will be sufficient to place the feasibility of large scale manufacture beyond any doubt.

On 19 June 1970, Dr. Vorster, Prime Minister of South Africa, announced that South African scientists had developed a new process for the enrichment of uranium and that a pilot plant was being built. It was a breakthrough "unequalled in South African history" and was directed "entirely to peaceful purposes". Commenting upon this announcement, the Science Staff of the London *Daily Telegraph* said that Britain's atomic scientists were mystified. The Science Staff added that enriched uranium had two uses: "It can be made in the slightly enriched form as fuel for nuclear power stations and in the highly-enriched form it is used for bombs."

On 12 April 1971 the *Rand Daily Mail* ran a down-column inside-page story that warranted bigger prominence. The first half of the story reads:

> The Chairman of the Atomic Energy Board——Dr. A. J. A. Roux——says that with its uranium enrichment process South Africa is theoretically in a position to make its own nuclear weapons. Dr. Roux——also chairman of the Uranium Enrichment Corporation——said in a radio interview yesterday that it would be unpractical and almost impossible for South Africa to make nuclear weapons from plutonium. The reasons for this were that much of the material and equipment needed to make use of plutonium for military purposes would have to be imported from abroad. Such an installation would also be subject to international inspection. Although South African policy was to use her enriched

Earth Island

Earth Island Limited is an independent publishing house founded in London at the end of 1971 to specialise in the international publication of works dealing with a broad front of environmental problems urgently threatening our planet.

Strong links with Friends of the Earth ensure that a proportion of profits are used to support the work of that leading, direct-action conservation group in Britain.

Friends of the Earth

Committed to the conservation, restoration and rational use of the Ecosphere.

The earth needs friends. To become a Friend of the Earth, you need only register—and to help us as best you can. If you are able to make a financial contribution, your help becomes even more valuable.

Registration form:

Register as a Friend ☐
Friend & Supporter £3 ☐
Friend & Life Member £30 ☐

Name _____

Address _____

(Please include details if you have specialised training or knowledge.)

Standing order: _____ Bank

Branch No. _____

Bank Address _____

_____

Please pay on _____ (Date of 1st payment) _____

to Midland Bank, 455 Strand WC2, 40-02-08

the sum of £ _____

for credit to account of Friends of the Earth Ltd, 81001051

and make similar payments _____ (state frequency)

up to _____ (or until cancelled)

Date _____ Signature _____

Please send registration form and standing order to
Friends of the Earth Limited 9 Poland Street London W1V 3DG

uranium for peaceful purposes, the new process recently developed in the country put her in a position to make her own atomic weapons.

This new process, as I have set out to show, is possible because of the big new supply of uranium from the Rossing mine. The British Government and RTZ not only give moral support to South Africa's illegal rule in South West Africa but supply the racist regime with the means to make nuclear weapons.

NOTES

1. Ruth First, *South West Africa*, pp. 73–4.
2. First, p. 74.
3. Helmut Bley, *South-West Africa Under German Rule*, p. 86.
4. Bley, p. 79.
5. Bley, p. 83.
6. First, pp. 79–80.
7. First, p. 81.
8. Margareth van Eckenbrecher, *Was Afrika mir gab und nahm*, p. 213.
9. *Observer*, 17–10–71.
10. First, p. 178.
11. First, p. 180.
12. *Rhodesia Herald*, 23–6–71.
13. The friends of Namibia wrote a letter to Benn and received this reply on a postcard: "Thanks for writing. We never adopted the policy of trade embargo as you know and I encouraged industrial and technical links with every country I could. I think this is right tho' I know many people sincerely take a contrary view." 21–7–70.
14. *Financial Times*, 9–10–70.
15. *Africa*, No. 2, 1971.
16. Letter quoted in bulletin of the Africa Bureau, 3–9–71.
17. *Windhoek Allgemeine Zeitung*, 9–7–70.
18. *Windhoek Advertiser*, 30–3–71.
19. *Windhoek Advertiser*, 29–3–71.
20. *Windhoek Advertiser*, 26–2–71.

Part Two
AUSTRALASIA

1. URANIUM

It's no good thinking English in Australia.[1]
——Mr. Val Duncan, Chairman of the Rio Tinto-Zinc Corporation Ltd. November 1966

OF the seven largest companies listed on the Melbourne Stock Exchange, four are subsidiaries of Rio Tinto-Zinc. RTZ has not only shown outstanding enterprise and acumen in Australia's recent mineral rush, but has also managed to get accepted as an Australian institution. The company has achieved this esteem even though its mining activities are of dubious benefit to the economy of Australia.

The Australians, or "diggers", grew to nationhood from the wealth of their mines. As early as 1850, South Australia was exporting more copper than wool and wheat. Five years later there were more than 100,000 men at work on the famous Victoria gold fields. During these early years, the metals were mined by individual prospectors or by small groups comparable to a football pool syndicate. Even the companies that were formed for more elaborate mining and smelting obtained their capital in Australia. Lawyers, farmers, merchants or publicans would raise the initial capital, then sell shares on the many primitive stock exchanges. Until the 1880s, nearly all the mines in the continent were owned and worked by Australians. As the historian Geoffrey Blainey writes in his masterly book *The Rush That Never Ended*:

> In the Herculean task of financing tens of thousands of shafts and thousands of crushing mills, pumps, and smelters, Australians got little financial aid from abroad. Although Great Britain was the world's wealthiest nation and lender and a generous financier of

Australian public works and companies, she rarely invested directly in Australia mines. Her more speculative investors preferred American railway shares. . . . If Australian news of rich crushings and new reefs only reached London slowly and irregularly, the shares naturally could not fluctuate enough to attract the speculator. London's share market needed quick regular news from Australia's gold mines, and the linking of Australia and England by overseas telegraph in 1872, and cheaper telegraphic rates in the following decade, at last made Australian gold shares a promising gambling counter for the British speculator.[2]

From then on Britain became increasingly dominant in Australian mining. The gold rushes in Queensland in the 1880s and West Australia in the 1890s gave the London Stock Exchange the first two bouts of the mining fever that still recurs, with the same fearful delirium, in the second half of the twentieth century, when the names of the more spectacular companies, like Tasminex and Poseidon can thrill every share punter in Britain. The excitement of the nickel boom and the colourful personalities of its promoters distracted attention from the fact that the real mineral wealth of Australia had fallen into the hands of giant foreign companies, of which RTZ has been far the most important.

When Rio Tinto and Consolidated Zinc agreed to merge in 1962, both these British firms had interests in Australia. Indeed, Conzinc, with its old and successful mines at Broken Hill, was the biggest producer of lead and zinc in Australia. It had done well in bauxite and had just acquired an aluminium smelter. Rio Tinto had a uranium mine and was interested in iron ore. The merger married the know-how and local experience of Consolidated Zinc to Rio Tinto's dynamism and skill in raising capital. Rio Tinto-Zinc retains an 80 percent share in its local subsidiary, named Conzinc Riotinto of Australia, in which the Australian public have the remaining shares. In turn CRA has a controlling share in five subsidiaries——Mary Kathleen Uranium, New Broken Hill (lead and zinc), Hamersley Holdings (iron ore), Comalco (bauxite and aluminium), and Bougainville Copper Proprietary in New Guinea. Besides these the company has interests in coal mining, lead smelting, and manufacture.

The Australian subsidiaries of RTZ are housed in one of the tallest skyscrapers in Melbourne, Australia's mining capital since the days of the first gold rush. Almost all its staff is Australian; indeed, Sir Maurice Mawby, the CRA Chairman and father-figure, has been described to me as a "very Australian Australian". Appropriately in a country in which half the prime ministers have been miners or sons of miners, Sir Robert Menzies, the former Prime Minister, has an office in the CRA building. I hope, for Sir Robert's sake, that his rooms do not receive the faint but maddening canned music that permeates the building.

I am not concerned in this book with the inside politics of RTZ or of its subsidiaries abroad. Although attempts have been made in some Australian newspapers to make interesting personalities out of the company's executives, they remain organization men. Doubtless there have been hot debates in the boardrooms of CRA and its lesser companies, but these are of no general interest. This book is concerned not with the inside workings of RTZ but with its impact on society.

The chapters in Part Two of this book are concerned with the exploitation of four metals: uranium in North Queensland; iron ore in West Australia; bauxite in Queensland, Tasmania and New Zealand; and, lastly, a much longer examination of the effects of the copper mine at Bougainville, an island in the Territory of Papua and New Guinea. Let us begin with uranium.

The "cold war" in the late 1940s, when Russia and the United States were stockpiling nuclear weapons, caused a world demand for uranium from which these weapons are made. RTZ was one of the first to mine the great uranium fields in Canada during the nineteen-fifties; meanwhile its representatives and prospectors looked all over the world for other supplies of the ore. In Australia, the uranium boom caused excitement comparable to old gold rush days, except that the new prospectors carried a geiger counter strapped to their bag, or "matilda". When the Government paid an award of $50,000 to the discoverer of a mine at Rum Jungle, near Darwin, the rush began in earnest.[3] Old gold miners studied the ways to detect the new metals; men with office jobs in Darwin formed weekend prospecting syndicates; companies were formed for sophisticated exploration by light aircraft. Refugees from East Europe were prominent in this rugged life, which entailed driving as far as possible into the hills or jungle, walking or riding horseback for weeks and months, killing wild bulls and turtles for meat, seducing aboriginal girls for sexual gratification, and draining the bars of Darwin on return.

Long before their merger in 1962, both Rio Tinto and Consolidated Zinc had mined uranium in north Australia. Conzinc had been brought in by the Government to work the deposit at Rum Jungle, while Rio Tinto acquired a share in the great Mary Kathleen mine in Queensland. Since the first discovery of uranium in this area and the subsequent bounties paid to the discoverers, hundreds of hopeful prospectors had begun to range each weekend from Mt. Isa and Cloncurry, the old established mining towns in the region. In 1954 a party of eight men was prospecting near the old copper town of Rosebud, fifty miles from Mt. Isa, when their geiger counters started to chatter. The mine, named Mary Kathleen after one prospector's wife who had died of cancer a fortnight before, was soon world-famous. The eight prospectors were prudent about their find and in their bargaining with the company (Australian Oil Exploration) that bought it. The eight men sold an option over the prospect for $500,000 in cash, plus 20 percent of shares of any company floated, plus 5 percent of any ore produced. It was at this point that Val Duncan, who happened to be in Australia on some other business, bought control of the deposit "quickly and almost casually".[4]

In replying to Australian critics, Sir Val often reminds them of the risks taken by Rio Tinto-Zinc at the beginning of a mining venture. "I suppose it is natural," he declared in June 1970, "when projects are highly successful to forget the exploration risks and the pain and grief taken by those who went ahead with them and to wonder why the risk-takers are still the majority owners."[5] The risk in buying Mary Kathleen was reduced by the fact that Rio Tinto already owned a large uranium mine in Canada and already had a customer in the British Atomic Energy Authority, which was predisposed to buy from a British firm. Moreover, on acquiring the Mary Kathleen mine, Rio Tinto was given a ten-year "tax holiday" by the Australian Government. This concession, almost unparalleled in its generosity, was a virtual guarantee of profit over the next ten years. It was a prime example of Australia's readiness to sell her natural resources too soon and too cheap to non-Australian capitalists.

By 1963, the Mary Kathleen Uranium mine accounted for two-thirds of the profits of the CRA group.[6] The ease of extracting the ore from an open-cast mine, the ten-year tax holiday, and a £40 million contract from the UK Atomic Energy Authority had justified Duncan's decision in 1955. However, when the British contract was fulfilled in 1963, the mine ceased production and Mary Kathleen became a ghost town. In the mid-1960s the demand for uranium slumped due to the slowing down of the arms race, and economists predicted that the expected boom in uranium for civilian nuclear power stations would not begin till the mid-1970s. Meanwhile, RTZ could still sell uranium to regular customers such as the UK Atomic Energy Authority. But holding reserves of the ore in two continents,* RTZ could afford to select which mines would be worked to the advantage of the company and its shareholders. In 1966 when the AEA once more approached RTZ for a uranium contract, this went not to Mary Kathleen, the Australian subsidiary, but to Rio Algom of Canada. The contract called for the supply of between 8000 and 11,500 short tons of uranium oxide between 1971 and 1980.

Australian critics complained that as long as Mary Kathleen Uranium was inactive, its shareholders were unable to earn any profits. They asked if RTZ's decision to close the mine had been influenced by the ending of the ten-year tax holiday. They asked RTZ to announce the terms of the Rio Algom contract and to state whether Mary Kathleen had been given a chance to offer a rival tender to the UK Atomic Energy Authority. In an interview in Perth in September 1966, Duncan sidestepped the latter issue, declaring apologetically:

> Obviously it would be foolish to defer for an unreasonable time obtaining contracts for MKU [Mary Kathleen Uranium]——whatever the price of uranium might be. This is because it is a great advantage to shareholders in getting earned capacity as soon as possible. But we will have no friends if MKU is pushed into a contract at a very early stage on terms which subsequent events might show it would have been better to wait a little longer. . . . The UK has been pretty faithful to Mary Kathleen, having

* Now three, with South West Africa. RTZ may also be looking for uranium in Scotland.

provided the loan capital to get it off the ground and the first contract in the peacetime nuclear power program. In that context it is hardly likely the UK authorities will not look in a friendly way at this lusty child when they played such a big part in its birth and growth.[7]

In November, after completing the Rio Algom contract, Duncan returned to Australia and still more anxious questions. "We do not know," said the Sydney Morning Herald, "what opportunities, if any, were extended to Rio Tinto's Australian subsidiary, Mary Kathleen Uranium, to tender for a share of the very big UK contract. We do not know what the negotiated prices and terms were." Conceding that the Canadian mines were an older and bigger investment, and that Mary Kathleen, as an opencast mine, would be easier to maintain "in mothballs", the article went on to ask:

How will Rio Tinto-Zinc Corporation, with its power to direct the bloodstream in two continents, choose to allocate the future contracts? Decisions that are ideal from Rio Tinto's command viewpoint may conflict with the interests of the Australian shareholders in Mary Kathleen and the interests of Australia's balance of payments.[8]

A reader's letter suggested a few days later that failing some activity at the Mary Kathleen mine, the Commonwealth Government should review the tax concessions to MKU, amounting to more than $24,000,000.[9] (Although the ten-year period had expired, these tax concessions still affected the dormant dividends of MKU in the future. This fact made the MKU shares especially attractive to rich investors since the dividends from these shares could be set against personal income tax.) The Government ignored this advice but the Minister for Trade and Industry, J. McEwen, spoke to Val Duncan and later informed the country: "He [Duncan] has assured me there are good reasons for the initial Canadian contract, that Australia will not be left out and that substantial procurement of uranium from Australia will be made in due course."[10]

The Sydney Morning Herald was not convinced by these assurances, for it returned to the subject on 15 November. After pointing out that Australia had still not learned the terms of the Rio

Algom contract, the newspaper asked if RTZ had considered Mary Kathleen's interest in the prior negotiations: "Were the board of MKU consulted or informed in the matter at all? There is a common impression in the city that they were not. Secondly if Mr. Duncan does not anticipate MKU producing again before the mid-1970s——eight or more years from now——why is this company retaining £4·5 million of surplus funds, arising from its original contract?" (This question was particularly acute since the previous year RTZ had offered to buy out the shares of the minority holders in MKU at about $1·50, or less than half the present price.) The *Sydney Morning Herald* then challenged Blake Kelly (Chairman of MKU) and Val Duncan (Chairman of his parent company) to offer the RTZ holding in MKU to the Australian investment public, at a price, say, 25 percent above what they had offered to pay for them the previous year. "If not," the article went on, with merciless irony, "will RTZ quote a selling price? Just why did it seek to buy out the locals at $1·60? Does that ill-judged proposal now tend, unconsciously perhaps, to affect RTZ's attitude towards pushing ahead new contracts for Mary Kathleen?"[11]

For years the huge influence of RTZ on Australian economic life did not distress the Liberal Government, which was ready and eager to sell the country's natural resources. Then, in December 1967, Prime Minister Harold Holt was drowned and the Liberal Party had to choose a successor. After weeks of wrangling between the partisans of certain prominent politicians, the Party decided to compromise on a seemingly dull, docile and right-wing senator, John Gorton. He proved to be none of these things. In his short but lively spell of office, Gorton achieved a world renown by his all too public private life. A section of the Liberal Party backed by certain newspapers, set out to destroy the character of the man it had chosen as leader. Because Gorton liked his drink and employed a pretty secretary, he was severely criticized in the press. But his real offence was maintaining ideals that contradicted the *laissez-faire* greediness of the Australian Liberal Party. A man of scrupulous honesty in financial matters, Gorton required the same standards of probity from subordinates. A conservationist, he deplored the desecration of cities and countryside. A friend of the union leader Bob Hawke and other left-wing socialists, Gorton opposed the dismantlement of the social

services. But Gorton's greatest unorthodoxy was his economic
nationalism, in particular with regard to the sale of Australia's minerals. Before he was brought down by his own party, Gorton resisted
the power of foreign corporations, above all RTZ, with whom he had
two famous clashes. The first of these was about uranium.

In April 1967, less than a year after the argument over the Mary
Kathleen mine, the Australian Government announced a new policy
for uranium. In order to conserve the ore (with the aim of eventually
setting up Australian nuclear power stations), any company wishing to export uranium from deposits of more than 2000 short tons
would have to prove the discovery of a fresh deposit equal in
quantity to the old. This policy did not please RTZ and its subsidiaries in Australia. The Chairman of CRA, Sir Maurice Mawby,
declared that the finding of further reserves of uranium ore was not
likely to be assisted by a policy which restricted exports. And the
Chairman of Mary Kathleen Uranium, Blake Pelly, said that the controls would have the effect of delaying indefinitely the writing of a
new contract by the company.[12] In fact, RTZ was now able to blame
the Australian Government for the rather embarrassing fact that it
had switched its uranium mining from Mary Kathleen to Canada.

In 1968 the Australian Atomic Energy Commission allowed MKU
to apply for permission to export 5000 tons of uranium oxide.[13] But
it was not till August 1970, when the Mary Kathleen uranium mine
had lain "in mothballs" for seven years, that Pelly announced a contract for 2700 short tons for sale to a subsidiary of RTZ and an
unnamed US company.[14]

The news that Mary Kathleen might soon be reopened was over-
shadowed a fortnight later by a spectacular announcement. A
company called Queensland Mines claimed the discovery at Nabarlek, in the Northern Territory, of an almost fabulous mine. It was
claimed at the time, and believed for almost a year, that the average
grade of Nabarlek ore was 540 lb to the ton, compared to a world
average of about 3 lb and an average at Mary Kathleen of only 2·46
lb.[15] Later it was to be found that the average grade at Nabarlek
was far, far below 540 lb. But at the time, the announcement struck
the Sydney Morning Herald as "an event of first importance for world
uranium markets, and an unpleasant one for existing producers like
RTZ".[16] There was immediate speculation, never clearly denied,

that RTZ, through its Australian subsidiaries, wanted to make a take-over bid for the Nabarlek find. In the House of Representatives on 17 September, an excited Labour MP, Mr. Paul Keating, called RTZ the main threat to Australian ownership of the Nabarlek uranium wealth. He went on to say that the group's financial control of Australian resources was "almost unbelievable".[17]

Next day, to general astonishment, Prime Minister Gorton intervened. After talks with Mr. E. R. Hudson, who was Chairman both of Queensland Mines (the discoverer of Nabarlek) and of Kathleen Investments (its half-owner), Gorton announced: "We [the Cabinet] have decided that it would not be in the national interest for control of these uranium deposits to pass into other than Australian hands. We intend to guard against control of either of these companies being gained through purchase of shares by overseas investors."[18] The first clause of the protective legislation would impose a limit of 15 percent on the allowable shareholdings in either company by groups of overseas individuals or companies. The second would limit to 5 percent the holdings of any one foreign person or country. The third clause would demand the disclosure of the ownership of any nominee shareholding exceeding 5 percent.

These measures, which would be normal in most independent countries, were looked on by some Australians as draconian, even socialist. They were in the end quite superfluous, for they referred specifically to the two named companies involved in the Nabarlek mine, which as it turned out, was very far from as wealthy as had been claimed. The complex, even bewildering affairs of Kathleen Investments, which stayed in the news through 1971, are of no real relevance to this study. The significance of the Nabarlek claim was in provoking Gorton to try to defend his country's mineral resources. As we shall see in the next chapter but one, it was again Gorton——and Gorton almost alone——who objected to the influence on Australia of another subsidiary of RTZ.

Notes

1. *Sydney Morning Herald*, 4–11–66.
2. Geoffrey Blainey, *The Rush That Never Ended*, p. 100. This magnificent book is the source of most of my references to Australian mining history.

3. Ross Annabell's *The Uranium Hunters* is a lively account of the uranium rush in the Northern Territory.
4. *Management Today*, September 1970. This flattering article on RTZ has been reprinted by the company as a leaflet.
5. *West Australian*, 22–5–70.
6. *Sun-Herald* (Sydney), 31–3–63.
7. *Australian Financial Review*, 14–9–66.
8. *Sydney Morning Herald*, 4–11–66.
9. *Sydney Morning Herald*. Letter from John D. Druitt, Cremorne Point, Sydney, 8–11–66.
10. *Australian Financial Review*, 11–11–66.
11. *Sydney Morning Herald*, 15–11–66.
12. *Australian Financial Review*, 28–4–67.
13. *Australian Financial Review*, 12–8–70.
14. *Australian Financial Review*, 2–9–70.
15. *Sydney Morning Herald*, 5–9–70.
16. *Sun* (Sydney), 17–9–70.
17. *Australian*, 18–9–70.

2. IRON ORE

When Wilkins Micawber lost hope that something would "turn up" in England, he sailed with his family to Australia, where he prospered. Australian Governments for the last quarter-century have guided the country's economy in the same belief that something would "turn up", or as the Australians say "she'll be all right". The slow decline of the wool trade due to competition from man-made fibres poses the constant threat of national insolvency. Yet Australia has continued to buy freely and hugely abroad. She has not created her own manufacturing industries, so that the TV sets, refrigerators and air-conditioning units that are purchased so wantonly for Australian homes are for the most part made abroad or by foreign-owned companies. The high tariffs were introduced not only to protect Australian industry but to encourage foreign investors who want a protected market for their Australian subsidiary. For example, the Holden motor-car, of which Australians, are loquaciously proud, are produced by a wholly-owned subsidiary of [American] General Motors. In spite of her high standard of living, Australia should really be classed in the "third world" of "less developed countries", or whatever phrase is now fashionable with economists, for Australia survives by selling her raw materials to pay for her consumer goods. Above all she lives off her mineral deposits, which have so far been found, or in Mr. Micawber's phrase "turned up", just in time to avoid a balance-of-payments crisis. We have seen how uranium, during the 1950s, brought an unexpected bonanza to the northern part of Australia. When the boom died away with the demand for the metal, pessimists in Australia despaired of finding a comparably rich ore. Yet in the 1960s, West Australia was to enjoy the greatest mineral boom——mostly in iron ore and nickel——since the first Victorian gold rush. The "lucky country" had struck lucky again—like a spendthrift finding an heirloom in the attic.

The West Australian mineral rush, which was led by RTZ, also caused a major change in economic policy by making Australia dependent on Japan, which buys the iron ore for her steel mills. As a spendthrift (to use the metaphor again) would pawn his goods to the prudent Jews, so Australia has consigned her ore to the industrious Japanese.

West Australia and its capital Perth epitomize this happy but feckless land. Pub talk is of lodes, cross-cuts and ore bodies. Schoolchildren, during the height of the boom, would pool their pocket money to play the nickel market. The Perth telephone directory informs you that you can dial the following numbers for the following information: "Time 1194. Weather 1196. Sports results 1187. Stock Exchange Reports 1193. News 1198. Dial-a-prayer 216921" ——in that order of importance.

Speculators have won and lost fortunes on West Australian mines, whose supposed wealth was often quite imaginary. The atmosphere of the boom was pleasantly portrayed in *The Nickel Queen*, a fictional film that appeared in 1971. The heroine of the title is a jovial, randy widow who runs a pub by a desolate rail-halt in north-west Australia. Two geologists, employed by a mining entrepreneur, arrive for some beer and are overheard discussing a find on a nearby mountain. The heroine gets up early next morning and stakes out a claim on the mountain-top, obliging the entrepreneur to give her shares in his company. Unknown to her, he is a swindler, who has persuaded one geologist to "salt" the claim with extraneous ore. On the strength of these false finds, and helped by the publicity for the "nickel queen", the share price soars. The crooked entrepreneur and geologist arrange to sell the shares held secretly by their wives and nominees. The good geologist, who is in love with the "nickel queen", exposes the entrepreneur, who flees, only to find that his wife has vanished with the money and a lover. The chastened "nickel queen" goes back to her pub and her geologist. The film, which was scarcely a caricature of certain mining companies, broke box-office records in Perth.

British investors have long been fond of West Australian mining shares. In 1894, 94 West Australian gold mines were floated and sold to the British, whose shadier journalists and promoters, such as the rogue Horatio Bottomley, grew rich in spite of the bankruptcy of most of the mines. By April 1896, West Australian companies were being launched at a rate of almost three a day, while the telegraph line from the Coolgardie fields was jammed with instructions from London. The "Westralian" boom did not last long, but those who had got out in time remembered it with affection. As late as the 1930s, a plausible entrepreneur, Claude Albo de Bernales, floated eight large West Australian mines on the London Stock Exchange, which later had him delisted. All his companies had collapsed by the end of the war, when the British Board of Trade sent detectives to investigate his activities. But in Blainey's delicate phrase, "they did not prosecute the man who had attracted nearly £2 million of English money to Western Australian goldfields".[1]

The recent West Australian nickel boom, which was a stock exchange sensation, distracted attention away from the massive and far more important finds of iron ore. In contrast to some of the nickel promoters, the companies that exploited the iron were large and financially stable corporations like RTZ, whose shares attracted investors rather than gamblers. Nevertheless Val Duncan's decision to mine for iron ore at Hamersley was reckoned daring at the time and is still held up as proof of his political shrewdness.

The Hamersley ore and its discovery, Lang Hancock, are part of West Australian legend. This area of the north-west was not virgin territory; indeed, back in the 1880s, prospectors had searched for gold round Mt. Hamersley in the Pilbara region, finding nuggets of up to 500 ounces. By 1890 more than a thousand men were working this hot, dry tableland, but if they noticed and recognized black outcrops of iron ore, they passed them by in the search for gold. It was not until 1952 that Hancock, a Pilbara rancher, saw the unusual rocks from his aircraft. Next year he explored on foot and found the ore to be iron. He kept silent about his discovery because at that time, the 1950s, the value of iron ore was kept down by an export embargo.

The iron ore embargo had been imposed in July 1938 from fear of the Japanese. Most of the country's iron ore went to the steelworks of Australia's largest company, Broken Hill Proprietary, or BHP, although small shipments were made to Japan, Belgium and the United States. But in 1938 the Nippon Mining Company opened an iron-ore mine on Koolan Island in Yampi Sound, off the north-west Australian coast. Since Japan was already at war with China and had turned

East Asia into her "Co-Prosperity Sphere", the Canberra Federal
Government feared this intrusion upon Australia's vulnerable coast
line. Australia's fears were military and political rather than economic, but to avoid a diplomatic incident, she introduced a ban on
exports of iron ore to all countries—just in order to get the Japanese off Yampi Sound. The premier, Joseph Lyons, justified the embargo on the pretext that Australia was short of iron ore. In time,
this spurious justification came to be taken as mineralogical fact.

After Japan's defeat in 1945, the Australian Government maintained its ban on the export of iron ore. It was still believed that
reserves were scarce; moreover, Australians now so hated Japan that
they would not think of contributing to the revival of her steelworks.
The West Australian Government was so committed to an embargo
that it even refused licences to *prospect* for iron ore. Any deposits
would be awarded, not to the discoverer, but to a company that
could guarantee to bring manufacturing industry to the state. The
Koolan Island deposits, from which the Japanese had been barred in
1938, were awarded to BHP in return for a steel mill near Perth.
Small wonder that Lang Hancock kept mum about his discoveries in
the Pilbara!

The export embargo and the discouragement of prospecting meant
that little iron ore was found. This in turn fostered the fear that
reserves were scarce. In September 1957, the Minister of National
Development, Senator W. H. Spooner, announced that ore was being
imported from New Caledonia because of the scarce local reserves.
He called it "most alarming" that Australia had only sufficient iron
ore to last for fifty years.[2] A Liberal Senator V. S. Vincent, asked
whether the Commonwealth Government* would ask the States to
collaborate in surveys and exploration for iron ore reserves and in
offering bounties, similar to those for discoveries of uranium. However, Dr. John A. Dunn, a former chief economist at the Bureau of
Mineral Resources, said it was pointless to hope that the vast territory
of the north-west could be covered in detail by official geological
surveys. He reminded Australia that there were still "men of the hard
prospecting type, knowledgeable, and with ideas on where to go if

* The Commonwealth is the federation of six Australian states: New
South Wales, Victoria, Tasmania, Queensland, South Australia and West
Australia.

the incentive to prospect is there".[3] This kind of talk appealed to Lang Hancock, who not only knew of an iron deposit but felt a rancher's distrust of bureaucrats. Yet an anti-socialist Prime Minister, Robert Menzies, declared as late as October 1959 that licences would not be issued for exports of iron ore. The Government believed that "iron ore and steel were so basically important to the Australian economy that Australia's limited known reserves should be conserved."[4]

Only one year later, the embargo was removed. The reasons for this change of mind by the same government under the same Prime Minister are still not clear. The official reason, given by Senator Spooner, was that a recent survey had found bigger deposits of iron ore than had previously been suspected. This presented "quite a different picture" from that which a previous survey had disclosed some twenty years before.[5] The Minister of Trade, J. McEwan, said in December 1960 that the lifting of the embargo was quite unrelated to trade discussions with Japan but was done in the interests of the Australian people.[6] Nevertheless there had been a Canberra lobby of businessmen and journalists who favoured closer ties with Japan. They included Maxwell Newton, a financial journalist who at this time was in close touch with Maurice Mawby of Conzinc (later the head of CRA) about ways to remove the iron ore embargo. Many people have taken the credit for getting the embargo lifted; nevertheless one is forced to agree with Geoffrey Blainey that the main cause of the change of mind was a credit squeeze.[7] Australia needed money——and iron ore had "turned up". An Opposition member of the House of Representatives cried: "It is scandalous! You are selling Australia's assets!" and another Labour speaker, D. J. Curtain, called it a "criminal action".[8] Yet the embargo was lifted, not because of plotting by foreign business companies, but because the Australian Government and people needed cash to continue their spending spree. Many months were to pass before a mining company, RTZ, was persuaded to take the risk of exploiting the West Australian ore. It was the British, not the Australians, who grasped the importance of Lang Hancock's discovery.

As soon as the iron-ore embargo was lifted, Hancock looked for a company to mine his Pilbara find. He lobbied in Melbourne and flew geologists in his private plane to examine the outcrops of ore. But the

Australian companies were deterred by the risks of the undertaking,
the great distances from Hamersley to the sea, and the difficulty of
raising cash on Australia's meagre capital market. The largest Australian company, BHP, which consumed iron ore in its own steel
works, was wary of risks. Hancock approached Consolidated Zinc
but found them to be equally timid. In a recent interview, Hancock
was asked if technical expertise had not taken the risk out of mining
enterprises like Hamersley. He answered:

> I don't quite follow you because my impression is that nobody
> has taken the risk out of mining. If you'd been at the conference
> table with me trying to get CRA [in fact Conzinc had not yet
> merged into CRA] to come into Tom Price [the mine at Mt. Tom
> Price] you'd know there were risks. I did 14 trips to Melbourne in
> one year to hold their hands. Every conceivable kind of risk and
> bogy was put up against it. They said go away and find a deposit of
> ore on the sea somewhere and meanwhile go to hell because you're
> talking through your hat. ... They wouldn't come into it at all
> until I found who their boss was and he did take a risk.[9]

This was Duncan, who came to West Australia to see Hancock.
"When I heard he was coming," Hancock recalled in another interview, "I went to Charles Court [then Western Australian Minister for
Industrial Development] and I said, 'What is it you want that will do
the most good for Western Australia in your eyes?' He said, 'Oh, a
steel mill.' If he'd wanted gold knobs on three coffins I'd have got
gold knobs on three coffins...." When he met Duncan, Hancock
explained:

> ... "You have got to put something on the line. This thing has gone
> on for so long that the Government has got its mouth open wider
> and wider." Duncan said: "What have we got to do, what do we
> have to promise them?" and I said, "You've got to promise them a
> steel mill." He said, "Don't be a bloody fool, we are not in the steel
> business."

In the end Duncan did offer a steel mill in return for the Pilbara
concession. But even he did not act rashly on such a gigantic project.
The first step was to merge Rio Tinto with Consolidated Zinc to form
the present RTZ and its subsidiary CRA. To reinforce the iron-ore

venture, Duncan offered a share to Kaiser of the United States, who were partners of Conzinc in the Comalco bauxite project (see next chapter). Next he approached the Japanese steel men for assurances of a market for Pilbara ore, which in turn would provide guarantees for his own financial backers. As Sir Maurice Mawby, Chairman of CRA, was later to acknowledge:

> It was the willingness of the Japanese in the 1960s to negotiate long-term supply contracts for the raw materials needed by their rapidly expanding iron and steel industry that enabled development of the Pilbara iron ore deposits to proceed. The assured cash flow generated by production to meet forward commitments and the firm belief that the companies concerned would be able to start production as scheduled gave financial institutions the confidence to provide, as loans, the huge sums needed to get the projects into production.[10]

Duncan had once more displayed his gifts as an international broker. An Englishman, he had found the finance, largely American, to mine Australian ore with a guarantee of sale to Japan. Australians might ask why it had to be left to a British firm to mine and market Australian ore. But Australians who have heard of Hamersley probably think of it as an Australian company. The Chairman, the Managing Director, and most of the employees are Australian. A CRA official said in July 1962 that "the company to be formed to develop these Pilbara areas shall retain a strong Australian character and Australian control."[11] Yet CRA, which holds a majority share in Hamersley Iron, is itself largely owned by RTZ. The company has announced that it will, "in due course, establish a steel industry" in West Australia, but so far this has not been built. In return for its iron ore, RTZ pays substantial royalties to Australia as well as tax but the fact remains that Australia does not control the ore and its end-product, steel.

Duncan has predicted that by 1974, Hamersley Iron will be one of the largest iron-ore complexes in the world. Following the initiative of RTZ, other mining and finance groups have been formed to exploit the north-west iron ore at various sites, one of which (Mt. Newman) already has greater output than Hamersley. Another hopeful entrepreneur is Lang Hancock, who was a rich man as a farmer, but is richer still from the royalties for his discovery of the Pilbara ore. In September 1969 he announced the hope of founding a company that would use nuclear weapons for mining in the north-west. "We plan to set off an underground explosion at Wittenoon, about seven miles from the town, near the present crushing plant," he explained. "The use of nuclear weapons would enable ore to be mined at one-fifth the normal cost. The explosion itself would cost one four-hundredth of the cost of conventional explosions."[12] This adventurous plan, which Hancock hoped would be backed by CRA, has not yet come into operation. Nor has Hancock's plan for an Australian-owned steel mill.

The lifting of the iron-ore embargo has increased the role of the Japanese in Australia's economic and even political life. Two great corporations, Mitsui and Itoh, have taken a ten-percent interest in the Mt. Newman mine. Maruben-Iida has a financial interest both in Hamersley and in the Mt. Goldsworthy iron-ore projects. An interview given in April 1971 by Kumao Okazaki, the Japanese Consul-General in Perth, shows how the influence of his country has increased since 1938, when a handful of Japanese mined at Yampi Sound. Referring to Sir David Brand, then Premier of West Australia, and Charles Court, then Minister for Industrial Development, Okazaki revealed:

> Charlie and Sir David were having serious differences and Charlie was threatening to resign. So first I went to Sir David and told him if he had anything to say to Charlie let me know and I'd tell him. Then I told Charlie I'd talk to Sir David for him. I was the middle man. Things soon became smooth again.

The peace-making Consul-General went on to say:

> Without West Australia and other parts of Australia, such as Queensland and Tasmania . . . Japan cannot live. We need not only your minerals but also many of your agricultural products. . . . When I came here I had to point out to Charlie Court the importance of this area in relation to the Indian Ocean economic sphere. South Africa is a second Australia——they sell all their natural resources and import manufactured goods.* Now Japan cannot

* However, in contrast to Australia, South Africa has a majority shareholding in companies exploiting raw materials such as minerals.

trade with South African countries because of the cost in transporting goods, but West Australia can——if it has the goods. *That's where our know-how and your raw materials can be of benefit* [italics added]. Our people want to be able to introduce their know-how so they can raise production capacity and reduce costs.... In Japan we have more strikes than Australia but we never stop work.[13]

Early in 1972, Japan reduced her production of metals and cut back her imports of ore, including iron ore from Hamersley. Australia may live to regret her rôle in Japan's new "co-Prosperity Sphere".

NOTES

1. Blainey, *The Rush That Never Ended*, p. 316.
2. *Sydney Morning Herald*, 4–9–57.
3. *Australian Financial Review*, 15–10–59.
4. *Telegraph* (Sydney), 7–10–59.
5. *Australian Financial Review*, 2–6–60.
6. *Sydney Morning Herald*, 7–12–60.
7. Conversation with author.
8. *Sydney Morning Herald*, 7–12–60.
9. *Australian Financial Review*. Interviewed by John Edwards, 30–4–71.
10. *Australian*, June, 4–7–71.
11. *Australian Financial Review*, 19–7–62.
12. *West Australian*, 10–9–69.
13. *Daily News* (Perth), 29–4–71.

D

3. BAUXITE

THE argument about foreign control of Australian mineral resources has not been confined to iron ore and uranium. After the Second World War, which showed the importance of aluminium in building military aircraft, Australia resolved to set up an industry of her own. The announcement of the plan for a smelter at Bell Bay in Tasmania was hailed by the Sydney and Melbourne press as an act of Australian patriotism.[1] The project was to be financed by contributions of £1½ million each by the Commonwealth and Tasmanian Governments, acting through the Australian Aluminium Production Commission, a body similar to the British Coal Board or the British Steel Corporation. But by 1951, four years before its eventual completion, the smelter's estimated cost had risen to £7¼ million, an increase that had to be borne by the Commonwealth Government. By 1954, the activities of the Commission provoked the demand for an inquiry. The Opposition Leader, H. V. Evatt, claimed that the Commission was unable to account for £1,200,000. Representative Barnard (Labour, Tasmania) said that executives of the project were issued with open bearer cheques which they used for work contracts. He further alleged that £48,000 had been paid for the hire of a bulldozer to clear a site of 40 acres. He claimed that one high official of the Commission was linked with a contracting company.[2]

The Liberal Government was only too pleased to blame the faults of the Commission upon the inherent incompetence of a nationalized industry. By the end of 1958, when the Commonwealth had spent £9 million on the Bell Bay project, its annual profit was only £25,000 and its aluminium was selling for £45 a ton, or more than the price of imported metal. One of the weaknesses of Bell Bay was the need to import its bauxite, or the alumina which is refined from bauxite. This dependence on foreign, mostly Malayan, raw materials, was all the more regrettable when one considers that within a few years Australia was found to possess the largest reserves of bauxite in the world. They were explored and opened up by the British company, Consolidated Zinc, which merged in 1962 into the Rio Tinto-Zinc Corporation.

Australia's bauxite deposits, representing a third of the world's known reserves, are found by the Gulf of Carpentaria, whose monsoons concentrate the alumina in the surface rocks. The two peninsulas, Gove and Cape York, on the west and east respectively of the Bay, are daunting and desolate by the standards even of northern Australia. A few prospectors for gold had braved the mangrove swamps and mosquitoes of these shorelines; a few missionaries preached to those Aborigines who had survived in this part of the continent that the white man did not yet want. But the establishment of the Bell Bay smelter gave an incentive to mining companies to prospect for Australian bauxite, which was known to be present (even if not so far in payable quantities) around the Gulf of Carpentaria. As early as 1953, Maurice Mawby, then managing director of Consolidated Zinc, suggested that bauxite might be found in Cape York Peninsula. However, it was not until two years later that one of his geologists, Harry Evans, spotted the bauxite while searching for oil near the Weipa mission. "As the journey down the coast revealed miles of bauxite cliffs," wrote Evans afterwards, "I kept thinking that, if all this is bauxite, then there must be something the matter with it; otherwise it would have been discovered and appreciated long ago."[3] In fact these hundreds of square miles at Weipa proved to be the largest area of payable minerals ever found in Australia and may indeed constitute one quarter of all known potential resources of bauxite in the world. Their late discovery was in part due to the desolate territory but also to the apparent lack of a market. Even after the discovery of the Weipa ore, there was no great rush to exploit it.

Consolidated Zinc, which was not yet married to Rio Tinto, did not feel confident of mining Weipa alone and therefore formed a consortium with British Aluminium. The resulting Comalco still had to be coaxed into exploiting its bauxite reserves by the Queensland Government, which was obsessively and irrationally anxious to win industry to the state. Although the Queensland Mining Act demanded a rental of 10s an acre, or £320 per square mile, the Queensland

Government gave 2,270 square miles to Comalco for the peppercorn rent of £2 per square mile.[4] As recompense for this generosity, Comalco agreed to build a first stage refinery in the state. This was duly opened at Gladstone in north Queensland in 1967. However, critics pointed out that Gladstone was merely a treatment plant where the ore was crushed and put through a caustic soda bath from which alumina was produced. In the production of aluminium, the large-scale industry and the lucrative part of the process comes in the second (smelting) stage. Knowing this, Comalco suggested to the Commonwealth and Tasmanian Governments that it should take over the Bell Bay smelter. Shortly before the acceptance of this offer in 1960, British Aluminium withdrew from Comalco. "This has created its own problems," opined the *Australian Financial Review*——"finding a new partner to help CZ finance the project . . . CZ has had no experience in aluminium at all and must be presumed to be keen to find a helper who has."[5] A helper was found in the giant Kaiser Aluminum & Chemical Corporation of the USA, and Kaiser joined a new company bearing the same name, Comalco.

The selling of the publicly-owned Bell Bay smelter caused little comment in Australia. Few noticed or cared that a foreign company now controlled the largest reserves of bauxite and the means to produce aluminium. The smelter which had been conceived as a patriotic duty was now in foreign hands.

Comalco flourished during the 1960s. The Queensland Government, which had leased its bauxite at such a generous rent, provided loan funds to finance the Weipa housing which was afterwards to be bought by Comalco.[6] Although an early agreement required the company to develop a township and harbour, the Queensland Government ended by building both. The Government did not press Comalco to give equal treatment to Aborigines in the area. A university lecturer, Frank Stevens, wrote in June 1967:

Against the $28,000 for European homes, Aborigines are placed in aluminium hot boxes costing $6,000. The streets and gardens of the European section are laid out in desirable stretches of green grass, and properly paved. . . . The Aboriginal village has unmade streets and I doubt whether the water reticulation system would support a village-wide interest in home beautification. . . . Where

is the trade training school promised? Where are the employment
opportunities for the Aborigines? The company currently employs
15 Aborigines out of a total work force of 370 people.[7]

Thanks largely to Stevens' complaints in the Sydney and Melbourne press, these abuses were tempered if not removed. Such
critiques of Comalco were seldom heard from the Queensland
Government or press. By 1970, Comalco had established itself as the
largest, most vertically integrated and certainly the most profitable
of Australia's three aluminium producers; and the greater part of
these profits went as dividends to its foreign owners, Kaiser and
RTZ.

The Australian politicians and press had for years been kind to
Comalco. The gratitude of the company was expressed in Comalco's
public floatation of 1970, when selected statesmen and journalists
were offered shares at a most attractive price. This controversial
offer appears to have been conceived by the RTZ half of the partner-
ship, for Kaiser made no comment throughout the consequent
wrangle. The Comalco affair is interesting as one of the very rare
instances when an RTZ company has behaved with apparent clumsi-
ness in its public relations dealings. I say "apparent", for I am not
convinced that Comalco was too distressed by the reaction to the
offer. But first let me recount the story of the floatation and of the
arguments it engendered.

Comalco's decision to make a share floatation followed its acqui-
sition of a 50 percent interest in an aluminium project at Bluff in New
Zealand. It was decided that 13 million shares, or ten percent of the
capital, should be offered to the Australian and New Zealand public.
This was in line with the policy of CRA (one of Comalco's two parent
companies), whose Australian equity content had grown in almost a
decade to eighteen per cent——although, as Sir Maurice Mawby admitted on TV, the company still deferred to London on financial
matters. Of Comalco's 13 million shares for the Australian and New
Zealand public, by far the biggest allotments went to financial insti-
tutions such as insurance companies. For example, the Australian
Mutual Provident Society was allotted 789,326 shares, more than a
twentieth of the total. The 50c shares were being issued at $2.75 each,
but financial writers predicted that that they would sell for more,

perhaps $4, as soon as they went on the market. At some stage early in 1970, it was decided by Comalco that a small proportion of shares at par should be made available to individuals. These were classified under three headings: entitled shareholders of Comalco's major owning company, CRA; clients of the underwriters of the share issue; and a third group, rather vaguely described as "customers". The controversy was to centre upon these "customers", many of whom were politicians or journalists, and hardly customers of Comalco in any ordinary sense of the word.

During April, 1970, many individuals in Australia and New Zealand were approached by Comalco's brokers or by Comalco executives, and asked if they wished to buy shares in the new floatation. Some agreed and some declined, but none remarked in public about the offer until the end of April, when an article appeared by the finance editor of the *Evening Post* of Wellington, New Zealand. Mentioning that Comalco had offered shares to "selected parties", he went on to say that the identity of some of these "selected parties" raised disturbing questions.

> A large company such as Comalco has many commercial interests and it is only natural and logical that it should wish to associate some of these parties in its share-holding, where possible. But among those who have been offered fairly substantial allotments . . . are a number of men in important positions in the newspaper industry.[8]

The article also claimed that "a number of parties close to politics" had received special offers. After this revelation, the President of the New Zealand Newspaper Proprietors Association warned members that they would be well advised to consider any such offer in relation to their freedom of comment. The New Zealand Attorney-General, John Marshall, announced that Ministers of the Crown had made it clear that they would have no part in any share issue, and that if offers were made they would not be accepted.[9]

This news caused dismay at Comalco, whose spokesman disclaimed any intention of trying to influence journalists: "We certainly would expect them to write about us on merit, regardless of whether they took up the offer or not. I would be horrified if they did not. I have more confidence in the integrity of the Press than that."[10]

But the qualms of the New Zealand politicians and journalists were not, at this stage, taken seriously by their Australian counterparts, who tend to regard New Zealanders as too sensitive, even priggish, on questions of conscience and money.

The Comalco floatation might never have flared into a public squabble had it not been for John Gorton. As seen from his pronouncements upon uranium, the former Prime Minister is a strong Australian patriot with no particular reverence for foreign mining companies. Moreover Gorton was and is a man of scrupulous honesty in financial matters. Almost the only charge that has never been brought against Gorton by his enemies is that of making private gain out of public office. He is not a wealthy man and his very small shareholding is in listed companies, under his own name.

Early in May 1970, Gorton revealed to the *Australian Financial Review* that he had turned down an offer of shares in the new Comalco floatation and had instructed Federal Cabinet ministers that they should do the same, unless the shares had been offered because of holdings in CRA or because of a client relationship with their brokers. (In short, Gorton proscribed the acceptance of shares as a Comalco "customer".) In this interview, Gorton said that he thought it would be improper for any senior public servant who had been engaged in or was likely to be engaged in negotiations with Comalco to accept any offer from the company to invest in it. The author of the article, Maximilian Walsh, wrote that

> in offering the Prime Minister shares in a new company floatation——especially one that is bang in the middle of the political field——Comalco seems to have shown a surprising lack of sensitivity. This is particularly surprising in a company headed up by a former senior Treasury official, Mr. D. J. Hibberd.[11]

Indeed it was Hibberd who offered Gorton the shares by telephone.

A week after Gorton's implied rebuke, Comalco and its parent company CRA announced in a joint statement:

> In Australia it is accepted practice under the present method of distributing shares, especially in the case of initial floatations, for the issuing company to suggest to the broker that some of the

invitations be sent to particular individuals. However it is recognized that this could be open to misinterpretation when extended to individuals in public office. Both companies firmly reject any imputation that invitations were made with an improper motive, but state that they will in future follow a practice of not extending invitations to subscribe for shares in this way to any person who is the holder of a public office.[12]

This announcement was made on 12 May, almost a month before the Comalco float was due to open on the markets: that date had been fixed for Thursday 11 June. Until the last few days it was expected that the 50c shares, sold for $2.75 each, would open round about $4. Then, on Tuesday 9 June, the Melbourne *Age* published an article naming some of the individuals who had bought shares, and stating the quantity they had received. The names included Sir Henry Bolte, Prime Minister of Victoria, 1516 shares; Lady Bolte, 166 shares; Sir David Brand, Prime Minister of West Australia, 1500 shares; Mrs. Mollie Askin, wife of the Prime Minister of New South Wales, 1500 shares; Sir Roden Cutler, Governor of New South Wales, 1154 shares; members of Sir Roden's family, 1600 shares. Allotments of shares had been accepted by almost half the cabinet of Queensland, the state that had been so hospitable to Comalco in the past. The Queensland Premier Bjelke Peterson was not shown as a recipient (although his wife accepted a small allotment), but the state's Treasurer and acting Premier, Gordon Chalk, took 1500 shares, and other members of his family took 1500.

Some of the politicians named by the *Age* had been offered allotments of shares on the strength of holdings in CRA or because of client relationships with the brokers. Most were classed as "customers". These included Mrs. Askin, whose husband exclaimed the same day that her Comalco purchase was a normal broker-client transaction and there had been no approach from Comalco, in any shape or form. "My wife," Askin declared, "has bought shares, off and on, for years with her own money. Sometimes they have increased in value; others have fallen well below what she paid."[13]

On this occasion Mrs. Askin was lucky, for one of the consequences of publicity was that Comalco shares opened on 11 June at A$6 on Sydney Stock Exchange, or A$2 more than the expected price.

Any holder of preference shares who "stagged", or sold fast, would have made a profit of at least A$3 a share. Mrs. Askin, for example, with her 1500 shares, could have realized a profit of A$4,500. These big paper profits, available to distinguished "customers" of Comalco, caused jealousy among humbler investors. Even ordinary CRA shareholders——those who were not also friends of Comalco——were entitled to only 16 shares in the Comalco issue for every 100 CRA shares. They were understandably vexed to see people who held no CRA shares allotted hundreds or thousands of shares in the new Comalco float at a paper profit of A$3 a share. As the *Australian Financial Review* remarked, "... the stock market's image is certainly not going to be helped by the implication, however vague or subtle, that every investor is equal but high-ranking ones are more equal than others".[14]

The political implications of the offer of shares to "customers" was not shirked by Comalco. A company spokesman on 9 June issued a statement that should be studied with care:

> The politicians on the list were a tiny minority, nought-point-something of the total number on the list. We haven't tried to delude ourselves we could bribe politicians with a few hundred shares. We have too much respect for their integrity. We have all along said that the standard procedure in Australia in floating shares is to make a list of names to submit to the underwriters——otherwise the underwriters' clients might get the lot. We're not a new company. Over about ten years we've made quite wide associations with people in banking and finance, Government and the civil service. This time we expanded our usual list to include people who've said over the years they'd like to have a chance to buy any new shares we float. In any case, those who did accept have to pay the full amount. A lot of them have said "thanks for the offer" but haven't accepted. It all sounds naive, I suppose. I'm damn sure we won't be doing it again.[15]

Comalco had no need to worry, for there was no political outcry against their allotment of shares. True, Prime Minister Gorton said coldly that the Comalco issue had nothing to do with him or his administration——an implied rebuke to some of the state governments. The South Australian Labour Party Leader, Don Dunstan,

declared that it was "improper for Ministers of the Crown to indulge
in share operations of this kind".[16] The Queensland Liberal Party
decided in conference that Cabinet Ministers should not operate
shares or other investments while in office;[17] but Queensland
Premier Bjelke Petersen, who belongs to the Country Party, angrily
rejected this statement and blamed the Press for the Comalco con-
troversy.[18] The acting Premier of Queensland, Gordon Chalk, said
that his buying of shares was his own business and nothing to do
with Gorton's direction to Commonwealth Cabinet Ministers.[19] The
Federal Works Minister, Senator Wright, indicated on 17 June that
the Commonwealth had no intention of looking into the recent
Comalco share issue.[20] The argument was briefly revived on 18 June
when Queensland Labour Senator Georges named several Queensland public servants who had bought shares at par. "The shares were
in the nature of a gift," Senator Georges asserted, and the civil servants concerned had "abrogated their responsibility, compromised
themselves and placed themselves at the mercy of an international
concern".[21]

The argument over the share issue gave Frank Stevens the chance
to revive his charges against Comalco concerning its treatment of
Aborigines. He claimed on a popular TV programme that the company's 13-year occupancy of the Weipa Aboriginal Reserve was a
reign of broken promises. Basing his claims on three "sneak" visits to
Weipa, Stevens said that Comalco had reduced the Aborigines to "just
another bedraggled fringe group . . . A 30 percent differential in pay
between Europeans and Aboriginals existed until recently, when I
drew attention to it," Stevens claimed. "The company then reverted
to the terms of the original agreement, to at least give the ap-
pearance of equal pay. But the differential still exists, because
European employees get a company subsidy for food and living allowance."[22]

One independent witness, a journalist who visited Weipa early in
1971, told me that some of Stevens' charges were wrong or out of
date. Moreover, in April 1970 the Queensland Government had accepted 40,000 shares of the Comalco floatation to be held in trust for
Aborigines of the state. The Queensland Minister for Conservation,
Marine and Aboriginal Affairs, N. T. E. Hewitt, said that the company
had offered shares to all its Weipa employees, including 38 Abor-

igines. He said that the Queensland Government would encourage these Aborigines to take up their full entitlement, with financial help if necessary.[23] Evidently Hewitt was confident that Comalco was a good investment, for he himself bought a parcel of 1,200 shares.[24]

In retrospect one is surprised at the lack of public concern about the Comalco share issue. The story was off the front page after the first days, and few journalists spelled out its political implications. In Europe or the United States, the sale of shares at par by a foreign company to politicians and civil servants would cause a furore, and could bring down a Government. Yet few Australians who profess a concern for politics have even heard of the Comalco affair. The Australian press is largely to blame. It is common practice for journalists and newspaper executives to accept favours from business, ranging from lunch to free flights, shares at par and even good jobs. Even those who decline the jobs are bound to feel flattered by the approach and to regard RTZ as a sympathetic company. One journalist told me that he had been approached by a senior executive (whom he named) of an RTZ subsidiary (which he named) and asked to pass on political information that might be interesting to the company.

It would be invidious to name Australian journalists who accepted Comalco shares or favours; they are private citizens, not public servants. I do however suggest that journalists such as these can no longer write impartially of RTZ or its subsidiaries. One financial writer, who had harangued me for half an hour on the excellence of the company, admitted afterwards that its prestige was in good part due to the sale of shares to selected journalists. It is significant that the newspaper most critical of RTZ, the *Australian Financial Review*, forbade its editorial staff to buy shares in the Comalco float.

It was the *Australian Financial Review* that later gave front-page prominence to a forceful and erudite critique of the Comalco share issue by Dr. A. R. Hall, an economist at the Australian National University. His thesis was that the selling by foreign companies of a minority interest in Australia, although profitable to the company and to those who could stag their preference shares, was generally harmful to the Australian economy and a misallocation of scarce Australian risk capital. Dr. Hall even suggested (ironically?) that the argument over the issue of shares to politicians was "a clever device for distracting attention from the lack of benefit which the issue contributed to the Australian economy".[*25]

NOTES

1. *Mail* (Sydney), 21–5–53.
2. *Sydney Morning Herald*, 15–10–54.
3. Quoted in Blainey, *The Rush That Never Ended*, pp. 340–1.
4. *Tribune* (Sydney), 11–12–57.
5. *Australian Financial Review*, 29–9–60.
6. *National Times*, 7–6–71.
7. *Australian Financial Review*, 6–6–67.
8. *Australian Financial Review*, 16–4–70.
9. *Australian Financial Review*, 20–4–70.
10. *Australian Financial Review*, 30–4–70.
11. *Australian Financial Review*, 4–5–70.
12. *Sydney Morning Herald*, 13–5–70.
13. *Sun*, 9–6–70.
14. *Australian Financial Review*, 10–6–70.
15. *Telegraph*, 10–6–70.
16. *Australian Financial Review*, 10–6–70.
17. *Australian*, 15–6–70.
18. *Australian*, 16–6–70.
19. *Sun*, 9–6–70.
20. *Australian Financial Review*, 18–6–70.
21. *Australian Financial Review*, 19–6–70.
22. *Mirror* (Sydney), 10–6–70.
23. *Sydney Morning Herald*, 24–4–70.
24. *Australian Financial Review*, 10–6–70.
25. *Australian Financial Review*, 15–3–71.

* This article is reprinted in full as Appendix A, with the kind permission of Dr. Hall and the *Australian Financial Review*.

4. COPPER

THE copper mine on Bougainville, a South Pacific island, has been described by Sir Val Duncan, Chairman of Rio Tinto-Zinc, as the "jewel in our crown".[1] The columnist "Lodestar" in the *Financial Times* used a different but just as lyrical metaphor: "In looking at copper, almost certainly the element in the four major base metals which has the most assured future, there is no doubt that in the eye of the public both down under and on this side of the world the brightest potential star in the firmament is the Rio Tinto-Zinc Corporation's Bougainville prospect. ...."[2] A company prospectus issued in May 1971 gave an estimate of reserves at about 900 million tons, or more than that of the entire Zambian copperbelt. Averaging 0·48 percent of copper——the ore contains some gold into the bargain. The excavation, refining and shipping of this ore to the smelters of Japan could bring great profit over the next 20 years to the shareholders of RTZ——at the cost of damage to the physical, social and spiritual well-being of Bougainville, which, until the mine came, was a peaceful and prosperous island. Moreover there is a danger that arguments over the ownership of the mine could cause political strife, even civil war, in this part of the South Pacific.

Bougainville is part of the Territory of Papua and New Guinea, which includes the eastern half of the main island. Papua, in the south-east part of the main island, was a British colony before it was handed to Australia after the First World War. The north-west part of the main island, together with smaller islands like New Britain, New Ireland and Bougainville, were part of the German colony of New Guinea, which later became a League of Nations mandate under Australian administration. It will be noticed that South West Africa, where RTZ has a uranium mine, and Bougainville, where it has a copper mine, are both former German territories over which the United Nations claims control. However, in South West Africa, where the South African government rejects the United Nations claim, RTZ can operate behind a curtain of secrecy. In Bougainville, where the Australian government is answerable to the United Nations, RTZ has to operate in the open. On Bougainville, in contrast to South West Africa, an English visitor such as myself is free to ask this English mining company, its employees, and the local inhabitants about pay scales, housing, race relations and the effect of the mine on the community.

The problems of Bougainville cannot be divorced from those of Papua and New Guinea as a whole. The colonial powers arrived late in this area, whose main island is mountainous, densely covered with vegetation, and crossed by torrents and ravines that daunted the first explorers. The Dutch took the western part, which has since been incorporated in Indonesia, the former Dutch East Indies. During the 1880s, German traders and missionaries came to the north-east part of the main island and to the archipelagoes to the east. New South Wales and Queensland, then separate British colonies, urged the mother country to annex eastern New Guinea for the security of Australia. Indeed, Queensland sent officials to raise the Union Jack at Port Moresby, now the capital of Papua and New Guinea. But the British suspected, with excellent cause, that the Queenslanders were interested in the area for "blackbirding", the press-ganging of native labour for work on the Queensland sugar plantations. The British did not take Papua until 1888.

After the First World War, the administration in Papua maintained the British colonial policy, which was considerate of the natives; but in New Guinea to the north, the new Australian rulers, under League of Nations mandate, continued the harsh German system of government. The planters, many of whom were missionaries, demanded the right to coerce native labour. To quote Dr. L. O. Mair, the leading authority on the territory: "New Guinea residents, pinning their faith on 'bashing the coons' as the only sound basis of race relations, regarded the 'humanitarian' attitude of Papuans as pure hypocrisy."[3] The simplified English or "pidgin" which had been introduced by the Germans because they thought it unsuitable for the natives to understand German was supplemented by purely Australian phrases. For instance, on air flights in the Territory today, the hostess will first explain in English the safety proceedings in case the plane crashes. Then turning to the native passengers on the "bolus" (literally "bird"), she begins: "Supposing bolus he bugger up. . . ." This curious English is spoken more widely in former German New Guinea than in Papua, which was a British colony.

Papua and New Guinea comprise all kinds of races and cultures. The stone-age figures, with squashed faces and bones through the nose, that appear in the postcards and colour supplements are by no means typical of the island. The Sepik river people, magnificent sculptors in wood, look oddly semitic. Some of the highlanders are red-skinned and are so called by the black, handsome Melanesians of Bougainville and the other small islands. Hostility between the whites of Papua and New Guinea has been passed on to the natives.

The Second World War, in which Japanese and Allies fought throughout Papua and New Guinea, caused further unrest to the natives. Some sided with the Japanese. Thousands fled their ancestral lands for the white men's towns. The sight of food and supplies being flown in by plane or unloaded from ships encouraged the "cargo cults" which have characterized New Guinea since the arrival of the white man. According to this belief the Europeans obtain their "cargo" or goods through Christianity but they refuse to reveal their secret to the people of Papua and New Guinea. One tribe built a wooden "bolus" or aeroplane on a hilltop to attract the white man's aeroplane and its cargo.[4]

Australians have been dominant in New Guinea's economic life. The trading firm Burns Philp, founded in 1883, has expanded into plantations, hotels, retailing and shipping. Two other Australian companies help to keep a grip on commercial life in spite of rivalry from Japan and the United States. A New Guinea gold rush, beginning in 1926 at Edie Creek, attracted 600 Europeans and thousands of contract native labourers, many of whom perished from cold and disease in the highlands. Throughout the 1930s, the League of Nations complained in vain of the evils of the contracting system authorized by the Australian Government.

Since the war, the Territory has been expensive to the Canberra Government and to the taxpayer, but profitable to private Australian businessmen. Construction companies, service industries, brewers, bottlers and car salesmen flourish in towns like Port Moresby, Lae and Rabaul. In 1962, the UN Visiting Mission urged the Australian Government to train more natives to take on the work of commerce and government. It requested the Government to "cease its courtship of speculative capitalists who might be tempted to investigate and invest in New Guinea."[5] The Australian Government has in fact encouraged these speculative capitalists. Since 1962, when the UN made that report, the white, largely Australian population of Papua and New Guinea has risen from 34,000 to well over 50,000. Australia's exploitation is exemplified by the Territory's airline system, run by Ansett and TAA, the same companies that divide most of the traffic within Australia. On the flight from Port Moresby (the most crowded, uncomfortable and ill-run airport that I have ever seen in a lifetime of travelling) to Bougainville (where my luggage was lost), the two airlines operate a first-class-only service, charging full IATA rates, in spite of the fact that there is no extra leg space, no free drink, and a second-class baggage allowance. These all-first-class flights are now by Friendship aircraft but used to be run in ancient piston planes with canvas seats along the sides. Since most flights in Papua and New Guinea are full, a pleasant profit must be made by Ansett and by TAA, a state-owned Australian airline.

Papua and New Guinea have a measure of self-government through the elective House of Assembly at Port Moresby. There is talk of formal self-government by the middle of the 1970s, but this is likely to rest on Australian approval. The Australians fear, or affect to fear, a military threat from the north through New Guinea. Moreover, they are unlikely to subsidize Papua and New Guinea without maintaining control of industry, business, and agriculture. Even so, many Australians complain of the wind of change. "The administration's all rat-shit," said a Melbourne suburban car salesman turned old colonial hand, "they're all on the side of the coons, and the reason is they've got Canberra behind them, and Canberra has the United Nations behind it which is dominated by the black bloc and the Communist bloc."

Bougainville was named after the French explorer who sighted it in 1768, but it is now pronounced *Boganvill* by Australians. During the nineteenth century, the islanders were supposed to be savage——but not much more savage than their visitors. A famous Queensland "blackbirder", Dr. James Patrick Murray, kidnapped 80 Bougainville

men after sinking their canoes with scrap iron and small cannons tied
to lengths of rope. When the captives tried to escape from the ship
by lighting coconut fibre, Murray and his shipmates fired into the
hold, killing at least 70 natives, while Murray sang "Marching
through Georgia"——followed by prayers.[6] Although Murray was an
exceptional villain, his kind gave the white man a bad name throughout Melanesia. Geographically and ethnically, Bougainville is a part
of the Solomon Islands, whose southern part is now the British Solomon Island Protectorate. Indeed, when the British and Germans divided this area at the end of the nineteenth century, the British got the
Shortlands Islands only a few miles south of Bougainville.

It was from the Shortland Islands that Catholic missionaries set up
a station close to the present town of Kieta about the turn of the
century. The religion took hold until there were 30 missions on Bougainville and on the little island of Buka to the north of it. German
settlers started cocoa and copra plantations along the east coast but
did not venture far into the mountains of the interior. Although
"Buka boys" were valued as servants for their intelligence, the
Germans regarded Bougainville as the most intractable part of their
colony. Cargo cults started in Bougainville as early as 1904. Forced
on to German plantations, the natives complained of "No kaikai
(food), no Sunday, plenty fight, plenty die."[7]

The Australian rule that followed the German rule was not much
more popular with the people of Bougainville. When the Japanese
invaded in 1942, the people of Kieta, calling themselves "black
Dogs", threw in their lot with the newcomers to hunt down Europeans and Chinese. In spite of this persecution, two Australians managed to stay as coast-watchers and warned of the Japanese attempt
to retake Guadalcanal. This intelligence, said US commander Admiral
Halsey, saved Guadalcanal, and Guadalcanal saved the South Pacific.
But even this Allied victory did not impress the Bougainville natives,
who saw the situation unchanged except for an even greater influx of
Japanese. "They were well liked and they behaved themselves," I was
told by an official. "Do you notice that you scarcely ever see a person
of mixed Japanese blood?"

Resentment against the Australians persisted after the war.
Missionaries, mostly from Europe, remained responsible for education, and in the Kieta sub-district, forming the central third of the

island, the administration did not open a school until 1961. When a
UN mission visited Kieta in the following year, several Nasioi (the
main local tribe) complained of being treated like dogs by the Australians, and asked for America to take over Bougainville. Trouble
flared at about the same time in the northern part of Bougainville
and on Buka island, across the narrow straits. At Hahalis village, an
energetic leader, John Teosin, set up a "baby garden", in which attractive girls were available to the young men of the area. When the
missionaries protested, Buka young men and girls would fornicate in
front of the mission house. When the Hahalis rebels refused to pay
their arrears of tax, a force of 80 policemen was sent to Buka island,
where they were met by a thousand armed Hahalis villagers. The
confrontation barely passed without loss of life, and most of the
villagers who had not paid their tax were arrested and brought to
justice. But discontent——and the "baby garden"——still persist on
Buka island.

The Hahalis and some of their followers in the northern part of
Bougainville were accused by many Australians of creating a cargo
cult, in which they imitated Australian ways in the hope of Australian wealth. One of their leaders, Anton Kearei, told a visiting
journalist:

> I told my people that they must improve their manners, learn to
> speak English, and wear good clothes. Things like white shirts,
> shorts, long socks and shoes. . . . I know that some people have
> misunderstood my teachings, and there have been cargo cults. This
> is sad. When I started the New Ideas, I only wanted my people to
> be like Australians——to dress and talk like them, because when
> this happened we would no longer be ashamed. We would be able
> to talk and drink with Australians, and be equal.[8]

But the Australians jeered at these black men in white men's clothes;
they kept to the exclusivity of their clubs.

Paul Lapun, Bougainville's senior representative in the Papua and
New Guinea House of Assembly, told me:

> They call everything cargo cult but if you really listen to them
> they're not trying to get something for nothing——they're trying to
> get scientific knowledge, they're trying to get back the traditional

power to rule. When people saw their traditional chiefs beaten and cursed by the white men, they decided they were no longer chiefs. As for the baby farm, if we wanted to get back our traditional power we must increase our population. Many of them had been in Australia and seen King's Cross [the red light district of Sydney]. If they say it's traditional it's untrue. Nowhere did we have that practice before the white man came.... And why did only the white man get these skills of inventing and mining? If God is our father, why has only the white man got the knowledge to do things which the black man could not do? ... All these things put together come out as a cargo cult but it doesn't mean getting something for nothing. The main point is to get back traditional power.

Before the coming of RTZ, most of the 75,000 people on Bougainville lived by farming cocoa and copra, which is the dried interior of the coconut. Prospectors between the two World Wars had found gold at Kupei on the Crown Prince Range and in the Panguna area, near to the present copper mine, but exploitation did not pay. It was not till the 1950s, when rising copper prices and better extraction techniques encouraged mining companies to prospect for low-grade copper, that Consolidated Zinc set geologists to survey these South Pacific islands. One geologist, on his way back to Australia from a holiday in Japan, stopped at Cebu Island in the Philippines to look at the Atlas mine. Noting the geological likenesses between Cebu and parts of New Guinea, he went to the Port Moresby mines department, whose maps persuaded him that a large copper ore body might be found at Panguna. In 1963, the recently formed CRA, the subsidiary of Rio Tinto-Zinc, started more detailed prospecting. The company's 300-ton ship sailed to Bougainville equipped with helicopter, laboratory, and modern survey equipment which had to be flown into the mountains.

By 1964, helicopters were beating in and out of Panguna valley; prospectors were diamond-drilling deep into the rock; a make-shift, precipitous road had been cut to Kieta to take the giant trucks. From the neighbouring hills the Nasioi people watched this activity and wondered what was happening to their ancestral land. The RTZ men passed on this problem to the local administration, which worried about the villagers but knew that Canberra favoured the mine as a source of revenue for Papua and New Guinea. At this time RTZ was operating under prospecting licences of two years' duration granted under the 1928 Mining Ordinance, which did not require the natives' permission to search their land. In June 1966 the Territorial Administration rushed in an amendment to the Ordinance providing for large-scale exploration and production over an area up to 10,000 square miles. The bill restated the previous legal position that ownership of all minerals was vested in the Administration, to whom royalties should be paid. The owners of the land would receive not royalties but compensation. Many members, led by Paul Lapun, insisted that the sub-surface soil belonged to the owners of the surface soil, and he saw no reason why Papua and New Guinea should 'slavishly follow the customs of other countries'.[9]

Ill feeling increased in the Panguna area. Villagers put up *Tambu* ("Keep Out") signs on their farms. At one village, women with children rushed at an RTZ helicopter shouting "kill us, kill our children", then heaped the aircraft with cargo so that it could not take off. At last 700 landowners refused to accept compensation or a compromise royalty. The Roman Catholic priests on the island, who were, and are still, largely opposed to the mine, deplored what they viewed as the high-handed methods of RTZ and the Administration. The Panguna landowners were "getting robbed", said Father Bernard Brosnan. "They look like getting $30,000 a year in mining occupation fees and royalties. They should be getting 10 times as much . . . the company will be getting plenty of money, there's nothing surer. The only losing ones are the landowners."[10] As the area of the mine enlarged, the company encroached upon not only the natives' lands but their villages and homes. "They'll have to be resettled," said company manager C. R. Bishop, referring to the Moroni villagers. "Right below their ridge, we'll be sinking an open-cut mine 4,000 feet long and 2,000 feet wide. They won't like moving, but it's for their own good."[11]

They did not like moving, and it is hard to discover by what kind of morality this change would be "for their own good". Both the company and the Administration ignored the fact that the Bougainvilleans were concerned not with money nor prospects of work but with the preservation of their ancestral land, which had come down to them through the female side of the family since the earliest history of the tribe. "Land is the bank, cash is something you get rid of," said an experienced government official. Another Australian said: "Hundreds of thousands of dollars are going out but they [the natives] are still just as conscious of their land as they were three years ago. . . . They see the women as the source of life and of land." The hostility of the Bougainvilleans towards RTZ was best summed up by D. Grove, Director of Lands, Surveys and Mines for the Territory of Papua and New Guinea: "They do not want royalties; they do not want money for damage caused to their land; and they do not want the occupation fees which the law says the company shall pay to them. They simply want the company to go away."[12]

But RTZ, knowing the huge wealth of the ore reserves, had no intention of going away. Having established itself at Panguna up in the mountain, it needed a new highway down to the coast, a thermal power station, a port, a European town, schools and a hospital. To construct these on the coast at Rorovana, Anewa and Arawa, a further 400 villagers were going to be displaced. In spring 1968, protest meetings were held in the mountains and on the coast. More than a thousand people gathered at Kieta. At Panguna about 200 stormed the RTZ camp site. Ill feeling was particularly bad at Rorovana, where Brian Middlemiss, an Australian plantation overseer, led the villagers in protest. As he told me: "Originally CRA (a subsidiary owned by RTZ) wanted 12,000 of the 14,000 acres of Rorovana land. We really set up an outcry when we found that a large proportion of this was to be used for a recreation area. Today it's only 1,113 acres——only ten percent of what they thought they would need." The Rorovana people refused to sell their land, which was then compulsorily acquired by the Administration. On 1 August 1969, a hundred police were sent to help the surveyors mark the boundaries of the land, but in spite of this force, 20 women managed to snatch away a survey peg. Four days later, police used clubs and tear gas to beat the men and women off their land. It is interesting to remark that among the people of Bougainville, black and white, it is the Administration, not the company, who are blamed for the bad effects of the mine. In the words of Brian Middlemiss (of whom we shall hear more later): "The people had no bitch against the company. The company was virtually the administration."

In August 1967, the Papua and New Guinea House of Assembly approved an agreement granting a lease to Bougainville Copper Proprietary, a subsidiary of CRA which in turn is a subsidiary of RTZ. One term of the agreement was an obligation by Bougainville Copper "to offer the TPNG Administration or a designated approved authority a 20 percent equity participation at par ... within two years of the granting of the Special Mining Lease".[13] The phrasing of this clause is of great importance and will be discussed more fully later. It has been widely understood to mean that as long as the mine continues, 20 percent of its revenue will go to the Territory of Papua and New Guinea, or an independent state formed from it. On the strength of this agreement and of the ore body, RTZ won orders from Japanese smelters for 15 years ahead, as well as credits and loans from America, Britain and Japan. A fine new road to the coast was finished in 1970 and "pre-production" digging, to clear the top soil, was under way in 1971. Full production and export was due to begin in 1972.

When that well-known conservationist the Duke of Edinburgh visited Bougainville in 1971, he spent five hours at the Panguna mine but made no public comment about its effects on the island's ecology. Bougainville, as I was told on my first day, "is just a construction area now but it used to be an island paradise". It is renowned for butterflies, big as your two hands, various kinds of eagles, and plentiful fish that can still be caught in the muddied Kieta bay. I saw no sign of mosquitos; there are no poisonous snakes on the island; even the sharks here have never been known to attack a swimmer. The volcanic earth is easy for farmers, and Bougainville is one of the few parts of the tropics so far spared cocoa diseases. It was to preserve these pleasant traits that the British New Guinea Administration, in 1889, introduced penalties for obstructing the flow of streams and for cutting down trees near the sea. Such penalties, applied today, would cost RTZ dear.

The first and most curious effect of the Panguna mine was on the local rainfall. An RTZ official explained to me: "Before, it used to rain regularly at one each afternoon. Now we can go for a week without rain and then it will rain at night. Or we'll get two days' rain on end." This change is attributed to deforestation on and around the site of the mine. Far more destructive to the island is the effect of the "tailings" or waste soil from the mine which has been dumped into the Jaba river that flows into the sea on the west coast of the island. Even before production began, the tailings killed off all fish in the river and silted up the river mouth. Eight native villages have been forced to move ("relocated", to use the more delicate word of the company).

By the time the ore of the Bougainville mine has been worked out, the elevation of the pit floor will have sunk from 2,700 to 800 feet above sea level. A big part of a mountain will have been scooped out and most of it will have been tipped as tailings into the Jaba river. The Papua and New Guinea Ministerial Member for Works and Mines is complacent about the ecological effects. He stated in May 1971 that "within this area, when the mining was finished, 3000 acres would be lake", a useless swamp area of 50,000 acres would be converted to pasture, and that "20,000 acres would be reclaimed from the sea, also for pasture". This statement was described by L. F. Reynolds, President of the PNG Conservation Society, as a "blatant distortion". He went on to say:

> The 3000-acre lake will be the result of a hole filling with drain water. It will be as attractive and productive as any flooded, abandoned open pit mine. The "useless swamp" is a breeding ground for many species of estuarine fish, large numbers of waterfowl, and possibly other undiscovered endemic species. It is now being "converted" to "pasture" by inundating it with thousands of tons of silty overburden from the copper deposit. In this process of altruistic conversion the fauna of a large river system has already been destroyed. The 20,000 acres to be reclaimed from the sea will consist of deposits of silt removed from on top of the copper deposit, introduced into a river which in turn will deposit it in Empress Augusta Bay. This silt, which is already present in large quantities, has damaged the ecology of the bay and will eventually make it uninhabitable to the majority of the organisms now populating it. Pastures, lakes, and rivers have only dubious value when heavily polluted with toxic by-products released from ore concentrating processes. How long will it take to convert this present mess to "pasture" and "lake" after the mining is finished 20 years in the future?[14]

When I raised this problem in Melbourne with Brian Barry, public relations manager to RTZ's Bougainville mining company, he replied: "Now, I get pretty snakey when I hear the conservationists complain about what we're doing to Bougainville, because I live in Toorak, which is a very nice suburb of Melbourne, and I can't go for a walk without stepping in the doggy dirt which has been left by the dear little doggies of the rich people. So why can't they worry about conservation in their own suburb first?"

In Bougainville, as in Spain or in Wales, RTZ tries to justify the damage done to nature by the compensatory benefits of wealth and employment. The main beneficiaries of the Bougainville mine are likely to be the shareholders of RTZ. In theory, dividends from the mine will benefit the exchequer of Papua and New Guinea, although even that, as we shall see, is only hypothetical. But the mine is of little benefit to the economy of Bougainville, and may even be detrimental.

Apologists for the mine like to imply that Bougainville, before RTZ, was a backward and impoverished island. In fact its agriculture, based on cocoa and copra sold through farming co-operatives, was a model of sound economics for underdeveloped countries. In Buin, on the south side of the island (which has not been much affected by the mine), the members of the Busiba co-operative thrive on the sale of coconuts. The hundreds of cocoa and coconut farmers of central Bougainville who were thrown off their farms to make room for the mining company had netted about $1·55 a day on an average 15-acre farm, compared to the $2 average for a worker in the mine.[15]

Moreover, the farmer got the additional benefit of his trees——leaves for thatching and nuts for food. I asked Bill Brown, a District Commissioner attached to the mining project, if the destruction of agricultural land for the mine had given a bad name to agriculture. "I think it gave the Government a bad name," he replied, "not agriculture. The Government had been encouraging them to go in for agriculture. Now there's less incentive to farming. The price of cocoa is down and the price of labour is up."

The company's pamphlets and prospectuses make much of the jobs and technical training now available to the islanders. Blacks and whites are jointly photographed operating machine tools, driving a power shovel, and picnicking in the mountains. The Employee Relations Manager at the mine, Colonel Kenneth McKenzie——he was until recently serving in Vietnam——was full of praise for the skill of the local workers. "At first we hadn't contemplated using natives to operate $600,000 shovels for ten years. But we tried one or two when Europeans were short and they took to it like ducks to water. Now we wouldn't think of employing Europeans"——who are paid three times as much as the natives for doing the same jobs. Although this differential was imposed at the wish of the Administration, which feared upsetting the local economy, it is accepted with readiness by the company. To quote Colonel McKenzie again: "Morally, politically and economically it's a proper and sensible thing to do." Two-thirds of the company work force are black, which is helpful "economically".

Even so, the mine offers very few jobs in proportion to its size. In 1970 there was a working population of 10,500, of whom 9,000 were construction workers. When the construction workers have gone, say in 1972, the working population of the mine will be 3,000, one-third of them white. Of the 2,000 non-whites, only a third will be Bougainville people. Asked about the proportion of Bougainville men to people from other parts of the territory, Colonel McKenzie told me: "At present it's about 50 percent. At the early stages we were recruiting wherever we could. But we'd prefer a proportion of 33 percent." (When I repeated this to Bill Brown of the Administration, he said he thought there might be some resistance on the island if BCP raised the proportion of non-island labour). The immense but "capital-intensive" Bougainville copper mine will provide less jobs for the people of Papua and New Guinea than did the gold mines of the mainland in the 1920s and 1930s.

The company likes to argue that Bougainville has profited from the side effects of the mine. Some people certainly have made money, but probably few were Bougainvilleans. The shops in Kieta, which charge extravagant prices (a simple pair of sun-glasses sold for A$15) are run by Chinese and Australian traders, while the Bougainvilleans, as purchasers rather than sellers, have suffered from the inflation. Two of the waiters at the hotel where I stayed, were working to pay off their debts, and talked longingly of the time when they could go back to farming on Buka island. Although the mine has much of its food flown in——the pineapple that I ate there was not local but

tinned——the nearby farmers have done well from the sale of veg-
etables, as the company spokesmen keep saying. The alleged popularity of the company with local vegetable farmers would have been
more convincing to me had I not so often been told by American
public relations men of the popularity of their army units with vegetable growers in South Vietnam.

Friends of the company have praised the generosity of the compensation paid to Bougainville people for land taken and trees
chopped down. The London *Observer* observed that the Rorovana
villagers "were given $37,000 (a fortune by Bougainvillean stan-
dards)", although the vastness of the sum seems less striking when
we read in the following paragraph that the company's thirty-six ore
trucks cost $250,000 apiece.[16] In fact the company has several
times gone to law to contest the rate of compensation awarded by
the Administration's mining warden. Indeed the figures for compensation were built up by a series of legal actions. A price has been
arrived at for coconuts of about $5 a tree whose economic value in
cash sales of the copra would be $2·50 but whose extra value lay in
the nuts as food and the leaves as building material. This price of $5
was not accepted by the company because the Warden in a particular
case ordered the compensation to be paid out in instalments over the
42-year period of the company's lease. This order, which apparently
had been made to prevent too sudden a flow of money into the
district, was on the face of it favourable to the company, which could
spread out the payments over a long period. But the company's
lawyer complained that the Warden had acted on an irrational basis
and had no jurisdiction in awarding compensation other than to
award a lump sum;[17] one can only assume that the company feared
that the payment of compensation in instalments could lead to
further litigation and the demand for a bigger compensation rate.

The damage done to coconut groves can be measured and repaid in
cash, but no court can assess the damage done by the mine to the
social life of the island. This damage was particularly severe during
1970–71, when as many as 9000 construction workers descended on
the island. About half of these were Australians, or rather "new
Australian" immigrants from Europe who needed quick money. Many
carpenters, for example, came from Finland; some Greeks I met
could speak "pidgin" but not yet English; and the Yugoslavs divided

themselves into Serb and Croat factions. "Discipline was fairly tight when they were just shifting earth," said an administration officer of these construction workers, "but it relaxed when the unions moved in and there was a danger of strike action. There's a danger that the 'indigenes' may come to judge all Europeans by these people. I've never seen so many long hairs in my life." A priest deplored their gambling and their drinking: "One man in the flats had five refrigerators filled with beer and the hard stuff which he was selling at ten percent profit. The police didn't want to interfere.... They behave like pigs, and I mean the whites. Some of them take a slice of bread and spread the butter on with their fingers." Starved of sexual relations, the construction workers drove to outlying villages to invite the local girls for a "picnic" in the bush. Sometimes they were driven off at spear-point; many villagers have now put up notices saying "Private Property. Trespassers keep out"; Kieta local council debated whether to introduce a law that any Australian wishing to marry a Bougainville girl would have to prove that he owned land in Australia.

Construction workers who saved their money could make about £1000 on a six-month contract. The work was hard, especially during the building of the hairpin-cornered road from the coast to the mining site, and on one occasion eight men disappeared with their 40-ton bulldozer over the edge of the precipice. The fragments of their bodies were found days later and stored, for want of a better place, in the drinks refrigerator of the Kieta Hotel. Several lorry drivers were killed on the first, provisional, road——inspiring a Brisbane newspaper to talk of "sex-starved heroes of transport who mark up each journey like bomber pilots marking up their missions".[18] In fact only 16 people were killed on the mountain road compared to the 40 killed by drunken driving between Kieta and Arawa.

The non-white construction workers were mostly "red-skins" from mainland Papua and New Guinea. Although they were paid only a third the white men's wages, this was enough money to get drunk——and many fights ensued. Most of the fights, and the only murders, occurred between mainlanders, but there was much hostility from the locals. "The Bougainvilleans were quite a well-behaved people," said District Commissioner Brown, "and they're quite

shocked by the lack of respect for law and order of the mainlanders."
In May 1971 a Papuan was stoned to death by highlanders who
chased him to a police barracks and threw rocks at him through a
wire screen window. A few days later, a relative of the murdered man
cut off the end of one of his fingers in a traditional gesture of anger
and then displayed the bleeding stump at the same police station.[19]
On Anzac Day, about 400 Europeans and non-white construction
workers stormed the Loloho police station after three men had been
charged with using obscene language. Most whites on the island were
critical of the policeman for lack of tact in arresting Australians for
using bad language in a single men's camp on Anzac Day.

In its drunkenness, Bougainville is like Palabora, except that the
whites and blacks get drunk together. On my first Saturday night at
the Kieta Hotel, the revellers were five deep at the bar in a scene of
medieval roistering. Most were "indigenes", hook-nosed highlanders
or Sepik men, coal-black Bougainvilleans some with afro haircuts or
flowers stuck in their hair, most of them drunk, or approaching
drunk, or "sparky" as the Australians say. Some squatted on the
floor, others leaned against the wall. Three "indigenes" were teasing
a drunk old white man by holding a dollar in front of his face and,
when he reached for it, passing it to the next man. "How can you
expect the native to feel any respect for us?" said an Australian
engineer who had spent a year on the island. He continued:

> What do you think they feel when they see people like that?
> They spend all their money on drink or on cameras——look at that
> one with a camera slung round his neck. Sometimes you'll see one
> with a camera in one hand and a transistor radio in the other
> although it's only strong enough to get Radio Bougainville. At least
> 75 percent of them are homosexuals. They sleep together. They
> can't afford the price of a woman. Just look at them! Can you see
> them getting independence? Most of them are in rags. You ask
> what effect the mine has had on them? It's fucked them. . . . What
> we've got to do is to make them want the things that we want
> them to have but if you gave a Rolls Royce to the leading chief it
> wouldn't be serviceable after six months. All they want to do is a
> little fishing. Yet I'd rather have that roomful of natives than a
> roomful of Greeks or Italians or Yugoslavs. . . .

Next morning more than a thousand broken bottles and crushed beer cans lay outside the bar in the mud, for Kieta, Bougainville's capital, is a squalid shanty town without paved streets. It was the thirteenth annual choral festival, and parties of children were coming from all over the island, dressed in clean blue or white uniforms. They were followed by lorryloads of shouting construction workers, some swigging spirits out of the bottle. "Terrible, terrible," said a priest. "Today, when everyone was coming to town dressed in their best clothes, my boys commented that the white men drive in stripped to the waist, in swimming trunks." As the choirs sang on a lawn behind the police station, the Europeans chattered and tried to take photographs of the local girls, especially those who had bleached their hair with peroxide. The local men tried to block the photographers; there was jostling, arguments and abuse——over which could be heard scraps of song——"I'm ready for the judgement day ..." or "Sing a merry madrigal, fa-la-la-la-la-la-la". It hadn't gone off well, said the same indignant priest.

The Administration, the Company and the priests were confident that things would improve once the construction work was finished and the whites had been sent home. However it has not been so easy to get rid of the non-white construction workers from other parts of Papua and New Guinea. Even in June 1971, when construction work was in full swing, there were between 1200 and 1500 unemployed Papuans and New Guineans,[20] many of whom had to steal or scrounge to survive. The tailing off of construction work means that the mine has created not only employment but still more unemployment in Bougainville. Worse, these unemployed are men inspired by a new taste for beer, western clothes and gadgets like radio sets and cameras.

Sir Maurice Mawby, Chairman of CRA, once dismissed some published criticism of the Company's role in Bougainville as "misguided journalese".[20] To counter critics and to improve its image locally, the mine employs three former colonels to work on community and industrial relations. "Part of our job is intelligence and propaganda," said Colonel McKenzie with an engaging smile. "We have three community relations officers in the island to live with the people and find out what they think of us." He does not think there will be racial tension. There had been trouble at Port Moresby because "public servants and planters are not integrationists but miners are a rougher type." This hopeful assertion is scarcely borne out by the example of the same company's mine in South Africa, whose white miners are far from integrationists, or even by its mines in Australia, whose employees largely favour a "white Australia" policy. Indeed, Frank Espie, the Managing Director of RTZ's Bougainville mine, is a supporter of this policy. He told an interviewer last year: "I think if we build up a large minority of Negroes or Japanese or Malays we would find ourselves in trouble. But we can easily afford to bring in restricted numbers of Malays, Japanese or Burmese who are at a cultural level higher than our labourer, so you are not competing for jobs on the lowest level as you are in the UK.... I think I'm fairly well informed that the Government is staying fairly clear of American or African Negroes and I think they're right."[21]

The company claims to have made its peace with the 12–13,000 Nasioi people who live in the area of the mine and the port. And Paul Lapun, who is now on good terms with the company, says that "the land dispute has been settled now. The people of Moroni have had good houses built by the company, but the social structure is not as good as it was. Many people are very sad about the land destroyed by the company. They still hope they will all leave the place."

A distinguished American anthropologist has been hired by RTZ to make visits to Bougainville and study her people. His report has not come out, so meanwhile we must make do with a paper entitled *Development Experience*,[22] a study of the Nasioi people by Father John Momis and Eugene Ogan, an anthropologist, both of whom had lived for at least two years among the Nasioi people. They begin by saying that in 1950 "in sharp contrast to the New Guinea Highlands, Bougainville enjoyed peace and relative social calm free from endemic homicide". They say that "even had representatives of the mining company been aware of the existing social situation and been prepared from the first to cope with it, they would have experienced difficulties in their dealings with the Nasioi.... Initial contact between the company and the Nasioi villages in the area which is now the mine site was confused by company and administration reliance on a single outspoken Nasioi who had, in sociological fact, no right to commit the community to co-operation with CRA." General opposition to the mine was overruled, quite legally by Australian law, but "because their wishes have been ignored, the majority of Nasioi today suffer, in varying degrees, even greater feelings of intimidation, incapacity to adjust to modern conditions, betrayal and even fear for their physical and spiritual safety than they did in 1962 when they demanded a change of administration. . . . In the Guava area closest to the mine site, one hears men saying 'the white man is destroying us' and women 'we weep for what is being done to our land'."

Referring to claims that the mine was bringing vast sums to the territory, the two authors remark that when the UN mission visited in February 1971, the Nasioi made the point "that all the money spent on development benefited only Europeans. We believe the truth lies somewhere between these two extremes, though perhaps closer to the viewpoint of the Nasioi themselves." Most of the Nasioi employed at the mine were young and single, while many would not work there for political reasons. The company's "eagerness to employ local people has been frustrated by the long history of Bougainville neglect, the company has found the Nasioi were largely uneducated, lacked specific skills and had little experience with regular employment". The public had consistently overlooked the fact that "many Nasioi in coast and valley villages enjoy much more direct economic benefit from their cash crops than from the copper project". Primary production had trebled over the last seven years. The average income of a co-operative society member was $360.

The two authors give an equally sombre account of the social effect of the mine: "Although extrapolation from incomplete census figures suggests that the Nasioi population between the age of 6 and 15 increased at a rate greater than 20 percent, primary school enrolment showed a decline of almost 20 percent." This was the result partly of a new curriculum but also partly of boys' seeing their seniors getting exciting jobs without having gone to school. Their attitude could be summarized: " 'We tried to learn the white man's ways and what happened? Our land was taken from us'." Improvements in health facilities had affected towns almost exclusively. "With one exception, the Nasioi receive fewer health services in the village, relative to population size, than they did six years ago." The authors reveal that drunkenness is as serious in work canteens as in public bars: "Whole parties of village men drink to stupefaction in the canteens, they return to their homes where brawling and destruction of property invariably ensues."

In 1971 RTZ announced that in the floatation of its subsidiary Bougainville Mining Ltd. one million shares would be made available to bona fide residents of Papua and New Guinea, not only the natives but Europeans who had spent most of the previous five years in the country. "This issue," wrote Berry Ritchie in *The Times*, "is itself essentially a public relations exercise like the share issues of Hamersley or Comalco. It is designed to assuage Australian economic nationalism."[23] Since Mr. Ritchie has become a public relations consultant, one can accept his special authority on these matters. Certainly, he was correct in saying that as a public relations exercise the Bougainville float was fairly expensive: "Obviously the issue will produce extra funds for Bougainville Copper, but this money can hardly be described as cheap. Due to the depressed state of Australian share markets the coming issue will probably be offered on terms more generous than would have been needed only a few months ago." However, the public share issue was designed to raise only A$19 million for the A$400 million Bougainville project; of this the million shares allotted to Papua and New Guinea people was only a small proportion. Even of these million shares, most would be allotted to groups such as local government councils and co-operative societies. The company hoped that Papua and New Guinea natives would apply for shares as individuals, not because the company needed the money, but because the purchase would win the good will of the purchaser. Within months, the company claimed that 90 percent of its indigenous employees had applied, most of them wanting their full entitlement of 200 shares at A$1·55. Prospectuses in pidgin English were widely distributed through the territory. In the Kieta and Panguna areas, near to the mining operations, about 220 indigenes soon applied for the shares,[24] although, according to Lapun, some old people declined "because they think that if they buy shares they will be helping the company to look for copper in other places". Since the average savings of Papua and New Guinea people with savings accounts is thought to be only about $40, few could take their full entitlement of 200 shares. It was widely rumoured throughout the territory that Australians were trying to use the locals as "frontmen" to get shares.[25]

There was some doubt at first whether Australian administration officials would be allowed to apply for shares. In the aftermath of the Comalco affair (see previous chapter), a company spokesman made an apparent apology for the offer of preference shares to politicians and government servants. "I'm damn sure we won't be doing it again," he declared. Moreover there is a public service regulation that prohibits employees from holding shares in any company operating in the territory except with the consent of the Administrator. This would have seemed to rule out the Bougainville issue, especially since it was widely believed that the shares were underpriced and would appreciate when buying began on the open market.

The Papua and New Guinea Administration announced in May 1971 that a way had been cleared for public servants to hold shares in the Company. The actual mining was being done by Bougainville Copper Pty. Ltd. but the shares were being issued by its holding company, Bougainville Mining Limited (Melbourne) which did not itself carry on business in Papua or New Guinea. The Administrator, L. W. Johnson, said he regarded himself as being barred from taking up shares, as were his deputy, the Director of Lands Surveys and Mines, the Valuer-General and the Treasurer. In his circular, Johnson warned that "where officers were involved in policy or operational decisions on the Bougainville project there could be cases of conflict of interest if public servants or their wives took up shares."[26]

On Bougainville itself the administration officials were free to apply for shares except for Bill Brown, the District Commissioner for the project, and the Land Warden. Let us consider more fully what this means by taking the example of an imaginary patrol officer on Bougainville. He has doubts about the influence of the mine on Bougainville. He may sympathize with local grievances against the Company. He is constantly asked by the local people (as all government officers are asked) whether they should apply for shares in the Bougainville float. Does he say yes, knowing the issue is only a public relations exercise, but not knowing whether the shares are really a good buy? Does he say "No, don't buy the shares"——in which case he may be marked down by the Company as unfriendly, and the Company might even exercise its quite legitimate right to turn down his own application for 200 shares, if he should want to make it? He is a poor man and will probably lose his job when Papua and New

E

Guinea gain independence. Whether the shares go up or down in price, the very fact of holding them is bound to produce a conflict of interest. When I raised this point with Bill Brown, he agreed that ownership of shares might incline people to look on the Company as "nice chaps", but he did not think the sum sufficient to be an influence. But if not, why had he and the Mining Warden debarred themselves from making an application? Why had the Administrator pointed out the possible conflict of interest? The object of the Company in offering a million shares to residents of the territory was to win their good will. This good will, especially from important people like politicians and civil servants, will be still more important if, as I believe may happen, the company becomes involved in a major political crisis.

Bougainville wants to secede from Papua and New Guinea; moreover it may well do so——with the backing of RTZ. Since 1898, when the British and Germans divided the Solomon Islands, the people of Bougainville have retained a feeling of kinship with the present British Solomon Island Protectorate. They have never felt a kinship with the Papuans and New Guineans, who are different from them in colour, language and culture. Secessionist talk was common even before the Second World War, in which the Bougainvilleans favoured the Japanese. An Australian Government officer who had served all over Papua and New Guinea said of the islanders: "These Bougainvilleans are anti-Europeans, anti-Australian especially, anti-Chinese ——in fact, just about anti-everybody. They just don't want us or our Government."[27] Least of all do they want the "redskins" of Papua and New Guinea.

Secessionist feeling became a real political force with the advent of RTZ. It was Lapun who insisted in 1965 at the Port Moresby House of Assembly that part of the royalties of the land should go to the Panguna landowners as well as to Papua and New Guinea. The Government Leader in Parliament, F. C. Henderson, warned of the dangers implicit in such a move: "Give them five percent today and it'll be ten percent tomorrow and ten years from now they'll want the lot. Mineral royalties belong to the Crown. They are for the common good——for the whole territory, not just for Bougainville."[28] But Lapun won his point and a 5 percent royalty for the landowners. The continued trouble round Panguna and later in the coastal villages provoked still further discontent and, with it, secessionist feeling. On 1 September 1968, Lapun and the two other Bougainville MPs met in Port Moresby with 22 Bougainville students. They later issued a statement asking for a referendum on Bougainville so that the islanders could decide on their future. In the proposed referendum, the people of Bougainville would be asked to choose between three alternatives: unity with Papua and New Guinea; independence; or unity with the British Solomon Islands. At this time Lapun favoured the third alternative: "We are not satisfied with Port Moresby's Government," he told a journalist John Ryan.* "We do not belong to Papua/New Guinea. We belong to the British Solomons."[29] It was a strange confession of faith from the deputy leader of the Papua and New Guinea United Party.

The secessionist movement gained strength in April 1969 with the creation, after a mass meeting at Kieta, of an association called Napidakoe Navitu, whose aim was Bougainville independence. The leaders of the association, Lapun and Middlemiss, soon claimed more than 6000 members and general sympathy in the island. Membership dues were used by the association to start a business, Navitu Enterprises, with Middlemiss as Secretary. It runs bus and taxi services and has purchased real estate. I was told by Middlemiss: "As soon as we've consolidated ourselves in the transport field we'll go into the accommodation and tavern fields where the big profits are. We'll be taking up shareholdings in taverns belonging to European companies with a view to eventually taking them over." The views of Napidakoe Navitu are expressed in the monthly *Bougainville News* of which Middlemiss is the editor. "The propaganda on Radio Bougainville prompted me to start it," said Middlemiss. "They refused to read out letters sent in by me and the association, or they doctored them. During the Rorovana land dispute we countered their criticism but it was censored." Critics of Middlemiss say that the *Bougainville News* is unfair to the Administration, and fans hostility against the "redskins" from mainland Papua and New Guinea.

Middlemiss claims that Napidakoe Navitu has the sympathy of 80 percent of the island: "People are coming up from the south [or Buin area] asking me to accept the nomination for Member of the House

* From whose invaluable book *The Hot Land* I have taken this and other quotations.

of Assembly. The paying membership is mostly round here [Kieta] and in parts of South Bougainville which is the main population centre." His claims were largely borne out by non-partisan observers. An Administration officer said that the Buin people definitely wanted secession from Papua and New Guinea although Navitu itself no longer caused much excitement. Another official, who knows the whole island very well, said that the Buka and northern people were much more interested in ideas than were the Kieta and southern people although these two groups were "much more firmly in favour of secession". Many European priests are secretly or openly in favour of secession. For example, Fr. Wally Singleton, a priest and former journalist who has been on the island 22 years, wrote: "The United Nations and the paternalism of Australia combined Bougainville with the rest of New Guinea. By its present demands Bougainville may appear to be playing the role of the prodigal son. The difference is that, this time, the riches rightly belong to the son. Now, the son does not feel greatly obliged to share his inheritance with his Melanesian brothers whom he does not know very well. No one can question, I think, the right of Bougainville to ask for separation from New Guinea."[30]

Most administration officials concur with Canberra policy that Bougainville must remain part of Papua and New Guinea. "The secessionists have no idea what they would do, where they'd get the money from, or what other territories they'd join up with," said one senior officer. "Recently there has been a new idea, I don't know who's been putting it into their heads, that Bougainville should not follow Papua and New Guinea into independence but should remain under Australian rule." District Commissioner Bill Brown, although opposed to secession, had to admit: "Whatever they say, the mine has made a big difference because now you've almost got a viable unit in terms of cash, if not of people." There are strong hints that the company would not be averse to secession by Bougainville.

Officially, RTZ favours Papua and New Guinea unity. Speaking of politics on the island, Colonel McKenzie said: "We've got to know what goes on. The secessionist movement is the one that interests us. If there was secession we'd go along with it but we'd be disappointed." However, from the start the company has identified itself not with the territory as a whole but the one small island on which it has a mine. An article favourable to the company in the Australian *Bulletin* points out: "Just as the shrewd and energetic public-relations team serving the other CRA companies has worked hard and successfully at creating an 'Australian image' for this basically foreign-owned concern, it is now busy promoting 'a Bougainvillean' image for the island project."[31] Administration officers on the island privately criticize the Company for calling the Company Bougainville Copper Proprietary rather than Papua and New Guinea Copper Proprietary. When Frank Espie has talked about the politics of the mine, he has been curiously vague on the secession question. For instance:

> So in the Bougainville context I've always tried to ask myself what will the independent indigenous president tolerate of a big mining company and we'd better start acting that way today so it doesn't come as too much of a shock later on. The first thing he'd want to see is a fair proportion of good jobs given to his own people, the next thing is meaningful integration in the towns and the third thing is that there is a meaningful amount of small business in the hands of his people.[32]

It is by no means clear whether Espie referred to a President of Papua and New Guinea or to a President of Bougainville. The public relations consultant Berry Ritchie, whose article in *The Times* has already been referred to, stresses the tribal and linguistic divisions in Papua and New Guinea.

> Pressure is building up for the Territory to be given its independence from Australia in five years' time——a possibility that will be strengthened if Labour obtains federal power under Mr. Gough Whitlam——but in no sense can it be described as ready for such a move. What would happen if independence arrives so early can hardly be imagined. Bougainville and some of the other outlying islands might even attempt to secede.

Since Ritchie has excellent contacts with high officials of RTZ, and knows their thinking, one can guess that the possibility of secession has also occurred to Sir Val Duncan.

The leading secessionists on the island, Lapun and Middlemiss, both believe that they have the support of the Company. The former has gone on record as saying that BCP is in favour of secession, a statement that was not denied by the Company. "I'm welcome now whenever Mawby comes," said Mr. Middlemiss——"but I wasn't before." The Company has hired the buses of Navitu Enterprises, and supports the *Bougainville Times* with advertising and free editorial photographs. In return, said Middlemiss, his company wanted to buy 3000 shares in the BCP float. When I questioned Middlemiss for proof that BCP were behind secession, he advised me to study the terms of the agreement set out in the Company's prospectus. The relevant clause obliges Bougainville Copper "to offer the TPNG Administration *or a designated approved authority* [my italics] a 20 percent equity participation at par in Bougainville Copper within two years of the granting of the Special Mining Lease. This obligation has been met and the Administration has accepted the offer." It is assumed that when the TPNG becomes independent, this equity will be held by the government of the new state. But what if Bougainville should then secede from the new state? To which of two legal states would the Company pay its dividends? Or would it then negotiate an entirely new agreement in the light of political change? Moreover it should be realized that in an island as small as Bougainville, the Company with its huge wealth and powers of patronage would exercise an authority almost as great as that of a Bougainville Government. In fact it would *be* the Bougainville Government, perhaps exercising authority through President Lapun or President Middlemiss.

These hypothetical arguments could become real and urgent. As Middlemiss remarked to me: "If Bougainville succeeds in seceding the world will be watching." The secession of Bougainville, if it deprived Papua and New Guinea of half its expected revenue, would cause political uproar in the region. There might well be demands from the mainland for an invasion of Bougainville. Confusion on the east half of the main New Guinea island might give the Indonesians a chance to invade. Further secessions might follow by New Britain, New Ireland or even by Papua. To understand the implications of Bougainville secessions, one should consider comparable changes in other parts of the world.

The people of Bougainville often compare themselves to Biafra.

Calling for a referendum, Lapun said: "It will be better than fighting each other like Biafra after Papua/New Guinea becomes independent." A white Australian asked: "How do you think they could run themselves? If they get independence it'll be another Biafra, no doubt about it." A right-wing Melbourne commentator, B. A. Santamaria, took the example of Biafra to urge "a loose federation of largely autonomous states like Bougainville, New Britain, the Highlands (and) Papua!"[33] The fate of Biafra is well-known on the island, whose Catholic priests collected money for the relief of their co-religionists. Moreover, while the war was on and Nigerian cocoa production was down, the world price rose, bringing three years of prosperity to the Bougainville farmers.*

But Biafra is not a useful analogy. In the first place, the population of Biafra, before the deaths and by war and famine, was fourteen million, six times that of the whole population of Papua and New Guinea. It was a nation breaking away from a federation, not the splitting away of a tiny community. Biafra's motive in breaking away was to preserve the physical safety of her nationals, who had been persecuted, massacred and forced to flee in millions from other parts of Nigeria. Although a part of Nigeria's oil reserves was in Biafra, the foreign oil companies and other big businesses took the Federal side in the war.

A better analogy with Bougainville could be found in Brunei, a tiny oil-rich state, that kept out of Malaysia, apparently with the support of the oil companies. Still nearer Bougainville, the South Pacific island of Nauru became an independent state of a mere 20,000, thanks to the richness of her phosphate deposits. However, Nauru has only the vaguest links with the nearest scattered islands and it had never been proposed that she should join in a federation.

By far the best analogy could be found in the Congo. Like Papua and New Guinea, the Congo was ill-prepared for its independence in 1960. There were also many small, mutually hostile tribes spread out over a big area. The secessionist state of Katanga in the south-east was backed by a huge foreign copper company, Union Minière, whose operations were hampered by the anarchic central government. No analogy is perfect, and it should of course be pointed out that while

* A sardonic Australian at Buin remarked to me: "What the cocoa planters here should do is to organize another civil war in Nigeria."

Katanga is joined geographically to the rest of the Congo, Bougain-
ville is separated from Papua and New Guinea by the Solomon Sea.
Katanga's independence was crushed by United Nations troops. Since
New Guinea (but not Papua) is a United Nations trusteeship, the
Security Council could conceivably ask for another military force
to end secession by Bougainville.

The Bougainville secessionists are not so interested now in joining
the rest of the Solomon Islands. Their leader, Lapun, who in 1968
had declared "we belong to the British Solomons", was much more
cautious in 1971. He said that the people from nearby Shortland
Island still frequently came to Bougainville, but relationships with
the more southern islands stopped with the creation of the frontier:
"Before that they were sailing around all the time. Now they've
become too lazy to paddle and they don't know how to make the
boats. ... When we started our independence movement, we had
many visitors from the Solomon Islands both here [Port Moresby]
and in Buin. ... The North Solomonese would be very happy to go
back to how we were before but the South Solomonese couldn't do it
because they haven't got the economic base."

It is widely believed on Bougainville that the southern Solomonese
of the British Solomon Islands Protectorate are eager to join with
Bougainville because of the wealth of the mine. I found no evidence
of this in the BSIP, which I visited after Bougainville. Indeed, the BSIP
is so much more prosperous and well-governed than Papua and New
Guinea that the southern Solomonese dread any kind of union.

The main island in the BSIP is Guadalcanal, one of the bloodiest
battlefields of the Second World War: the capital, Honiara, stands on
the beachhead where the Americans first landed. The author of *Tales
from the South Pacific*, James A. Michener, wrote of the Solomons in
a subsequent book:

> Americans who scoff at the British system have one stubborn
> fact to explain. Bougainville, New Britain, New Ireland and New
> Guinea are better islands in every respect than the Solomons.*
> Their natives are more susceptible to development. But those
> islands have been governed first by the brutal Germans and next by
> the confused Australians. When war broke, the German-Aus-

* Mr. Michener means the British Solomons. Bougainville is strictly a
Solomon island too.

tralian-trained natives killed missionaries, betrayed coastwatchers
and sold American pilots to Japanese soldiers, who beheaded
them. On British islands not one white man was betrayed. Not one.
The fidelity of the Solomon islanders was unbelievable.[34]

Guadalcanal today is immeasurably more agreeable than Bougainville, in spite of the latter's supposed wealth from the mine. At Honiara airport, the immigration men, customs officials and airline staff
were Solomonese, and far more efficient than their Australian
counterparts at Kieta. From the airport I went in a smart airline bus
on a wide, good road, past women and children who smiled and
waved at us, past fine houses, schools, playing fields and a hospital.
The tree-lined streets of Honiara are well-paved, again in contrast to
Kieta. Even a street called Mud Alley is well paved. Here people
travel by bus or bicycle, the sensible means of transport for under-
developed countries, instead of by car or on foot, as at Bougainville,
where there is no public transport and the roads are too bad for
bicycling. The clean, handsome housing estate near Honiara, with its
garbage cans and well-tended gardens, was far superior to Bougainville's native huts or even some of the European quarters there. In
Bougainville, I was frequently told of the benefit brought to the
island by RTZ's technical school. In the BSIP there is a far better
technical school run by the British Government, which (unlike RTZ)
has no real commercial need for native technicans. Drunkenness on
these islands is rare, although alcohol is more easy to obtain than on
Bougainville.

The BSIP costs about £2 million a year to the British Government,
which would like to discover minerals as a source of revenue. Since
1967, RTZ has prospected there, first for copper and more recently
for bauxite. The Japanese Mitsui company has bauxite reserves in the
Protectorate. An Australian subsidiary of the American Utah
company has been prospecting for copper in central Guadalcanal, but
the locals at first refused to admit surveyors. They became still more
suspicious when they were told the purpose of the survey.[35]

NOTES

1. *Australian Financial Review*, 17–7–69.
2. *Financial Times*, 13–9–71.
3. L. P. Mair, *Australia in New Guinea*, p. 15.
4. The film *Mondo Cane* had a sequence on this.
5. Osmar White, *Parliament of 1000 Tribes*, quoted in *Australian Left Review*, March 1971.
6. Pearl, *Morrison of Peking*, p. 18.
7. Mair, p. 178.
8. John Ryan, *The Hot Land*, p. 316.
9. *Territory of Papua and New Guinea Hansard*, 14–6–66.
10. Ryan, 331.
11. Ryan, 333.
12. *Territory of Papua and New Guinea Hansard*, 23–11–66.
13. Bougainville Mining prospectus, 11–5–71.
14. *Post-Courier* (Port Moresby), 10–6–71.
15. Interview with administration officer.
16. *Observer*, 28–3–71.
17. *Post-Courier*, 11–6–71.
18. So I was told in Kieta. I did not trace the original article.
19. *Australian*, 8–5–71.
20. *Australian Financial Review*, 12–10–70.
21. *Australian Financial Review*, 7–5–71.
22. A study prepared for the fifth Waigani Seminar in the University of Papua and New Guinea in Port Moresby. Quoted in the Australian press.
23. *Times*, 23–3–71.
24. *Post-Courier*, 10–16–71.
25. *Focus* (Port Moresby), May 1971.
26. *Australian*, 7–5–71.
27. *Ryan*, p. 336.
28. *Ryan*, p. 330.
29. *Ryan*, p. 335.
30. *New Guinea*, June 1970.
31. *Bulletin* (Sydney) article by Eugene Bajkowski, 22–5–71.
32. *Australian Financial Review*, 7–5–71.
33. *New Guinea*, March 1970.
34. James A. Michener, *Return to Paradise*, p. 157.
35. Interview with British administration official at Honiara.

Part Three
BRITAIN

1. BRISTOL

Into Bristol today comes the Prime Minister, Mr. Harold Wilson. The reason: To open a fine new plant at the Avonmouth works of the Imperial Smelting Corporation, which contains the world's biggest zinc refining complex.
——Leading article in the *Western Daily Press*, 10 May 1968, on Rio Tinto-Zinc's new smelter near Bristol.

The world's largest lead and zinc smelting plant——built at Avonmouth near Bristol three years ago at a cost of £14 millions——is to close for two months because of a mounting risk of lead poisoning to workers.
——*Guardian*, 28 January 1972.

ONE evening in June 1787, the Rev. Thomas Clarkson, who had dedicated his future career to the destruction of the slave trade, rode into Bristol to start his investigations in the capital of the slavers. On coming in sight of the city just as curfew was sounding, Clarkson had sudden qualms: "I began to tremble at the arduous task I had undertaken of attempting to subvert one of the branches of the commerce of the great place which was then before me." Modern social reformers, and especially conservationists, will understand Clarkson's unease: now, as then, a socially harmful industry may also provide a livelihood for thousands of families. By attacking an industry, whether the slave trade or a firm that pollutes the air, water, and soil, the reformer may put thousands of men out of work.

Bristol typifies this dilemma. I am mainly concerned with RTZ's Avonmouth smelter and with whether the jobs it affords are worth the cost of pollution. But RTZ is only one of the local firms in the same position. Indeed, by some quirk of history, much of Bristol's

wealth has depended on wasteful or harmful industry. Her wine shippers have flourished on other people's liver troubles. Her cigarette
manufacturers, hurt by the cancer scare, have diversified into less
medically dangerous products such as potato crisps. Brunel's famous
suspension bridge was an engineering masterpiece but proved uneconomic, and also irresistible to people wishing to kill themselves.
Today some 12,000 Bristol people depend for their livelihood on
building the Concorde aircraft, which is just as beautiful as Brunel's
bridge but much less desirable. The livelihood of some 12,000
families is subsidized by the taxpayer at £1 million a week, to produce
an aircraft that is insupportably noisy, possibly harmful to the outer
atmosphere, grossly wasteful of fuel, and so expensive in manufacture and operation that it is certain to cost this country hundreds
of millions of pounds more, even if airlines are foolish enough to
buy it.

The arguments about Concorde and the RTZ smelter have an
almost exact parallel with the earlier argument about slave trading.
A brief study of that debate will provide a historical background to
this part of the book. As early as the eleventh century, Bristol ex-
ported English slaves "particularly young women whom they took
care to put into such a state as to enhance their value."[1] Under the
influence of St. Wulfstan, Bishop of Worcester, the merchants of
Bristol turned to trading cloth for French wine, until in the seventeenth century there was again a market in the Americas for
slaves. Ships would leave Bristol for West Africa with a cargo of
cloth, gunpowder, rum and trinkets to purchase a cargo of slaves to
carry on the notorious "middle passage" to North America or the
West Indies, where the ships were reloaded with sugar or tobacco to
take back to Bristol on the third leg.

The enemies of the slave trade——the counterparts of our modern
conservationists——were the Evangelicals, like Wilberforce, Hannah
More and Zachary Macaulay, who also were jeeringly called the
"Saints". They employed young Thomas Clarkson to get facts and
figures about the slave trade——the numbers shipped, the size of the
holds, the food provided and cruelties inflicted. His inquiries in Bristol took Clarkson to drinking dens frequented by seamen: "These
houses were in Marsh Street, and most of them were kept by Irishmen. The scenes witnessed were truly distressing. Music, dancing,

rioting and drunkenness were kept up from night to night." Even allowing for Clarkson's sober and pious prejudices, the inns of that age were probably less well behaved than modern Bristol pubs, where technologists appear in off-duty tweed jackets and neck-scarves to drink beer and talk about motor-cars. Even Clarkson had to admit that the merchants and shippers of Bristol were not all personally evil or cruel. On the other hand, the majority of the town's pious bourgeoisie were against the Evangelicals. When the first motion for the suppression of the slave trade was put to the Commons in 1789, a petition of protest was sent by the Mayor, Commonalty and Burgesses of Bristol, and another from the Master, Wardens and Commonalty of the Merchant Adventurers. There were petitions from the West Indian planters, West Indian merchants and from the principal manufacturers, shipbuilders and general traders. Bristol hired lawyers and "representatives", or what would today be called public relations men, to advance their case and to plant pro-slavery articles in the more venal newspapers.

The arguments used in defence of the slave trade were almost the same as those used for the Concorde. Three-fifths of the trade of Bristol depended on it. The abolition of Britain's trading would not benefit the Africans (read "enemies of noise") because other countries (read "France and the USSR") would continue to sail slaving ships (read "fly supersonic aircraft") across the Atlantic. If the trade were stopped, our colonies (read "our balance of payments") would suffer, and Britain would fall behind in naval strength (read "aerospace technology'). Bristol kept up this blocking campaign until 1807, when Parliament abolished the slave trade. But strangely enough, by this time most of the Bristol slavers had turned to other forms of business (or "diversified" in modern jargon) while many now argued that Bristol would actually benefit from the ending of the slave trade. In 1814, the Mayor of Bristol headed an anti-slave-trade demonstration, at which shouts were heard from the crowd of "A negro is a man!"[2]

Bristol people are very aware of their shameful, slave-trading past. Many believe, erroneously, that there are dungeons under the city centre, where the water at high tide came up to the slaves' necks. The fact that Whiteladies Road leads up to Black Boy Hill in Clifton, is taken to mean that Bristol matrons went there to buy slaves at a market. In fact the trade was direct from Africa to the West Indies, and the only black slaves brought to Bristol were personal servants of the returning planters. But legend and guilt account for Bristol's touchiness, which extends by inference to modern industries that have been criticized by outsiders. In Bristol it is a blasphemy to suggest that the Concorde is noisy and a waste of money. When the Concorde workers came out on strike in 1971, the convenor of shop stewards sported a Concorde tie at the microphone. He told the crowd at one meeting: "As far as we're concerned, we're one hundred percent behind the Concorde project. We are more in support of the Concorde project than the management. I'm sure if I asked you to raise your hands in support of the Concorde project I'd get a hundred percent support." He did not ask them, but after the meeting, a very radical worker told me: "Yes, I'd have raised my hand. I regard Concorde as a social evil but we were on television and if I hadn't put up my hand it could have been misrepresented to mean that I'm against the lightning strikes."[3]

Modern conservationists, like the eighteenth-century "Saints", are a threat to Bristol's economic life. Its chronic unemployment grew in 1970–71 to serious proportions. Campaigns against the Concorde, or cigarettes, could, if successful, throw thousands on to the dole. The eagerness for jobs helps to explain why RTZ was allowed to build a smelting plant, whose pollution would have provoked far more protest in other parts of Britain.

The Imperial Smelting Corporation began as the National Smelting Company during the First World War when Britain could no longer import refined zinc from Belgium and Germany. The ore came from the Broken Hill mines of Consolidated Zinc, which later took over the Company. The merger with Rio Tinto brought exciting changes to this rather conservative smelting firm. As the *Observer* explained on 19 July 1964:

[Val] Duncan, the charming, 51-year-old ex-barrister Chairman of RTZ, started a considerable rumpus on Monday. He announced that his Imperial Smelting offshoot would abandon the hallowed [London Metal] Exchange prices and set its own——£125 or £14·15s down——on the going level——with the firm intention of dropping further.... In zinc, Rio Tinto's Duncan finds it very difficult to see what useful function the L.M.E. can perform.

The Imperial Smelting Corporation grew in the 1960s with the development of a chemical propellent, trade-named Isceon, which could be used in aerosol packs for shaving cream, paint spray, oven cleaners or cosmetics. Propellents and refrigerants such as Isceon are based on sulphuric acid, which in turn is the main by-product of zinc smelting. Partly to meet the expected demand for Isceon, the Imperial Smelting Company started work in 1966 on a £15 million project to boost production of zinc metal to 180,000 tons a year. From this it was proposed to double the production of sulphuric acid, for which ISC built a 75,000-ton-capacity plant. The centrepiece of the project was a £4 million blast furnace, controlled by computer. Indeed, Managing Director William Johnson boasted that it would be "the most highly automated zinc smelting plant in the world". The new furnace, which smelts zinc and lead at the same time, was also designed to save manpower. Imperial's old-style vertical retort plant needed 160 process workers to smelt 40,000 tons of metal a year. The new furnace could produce 90,000 tons with far fewer men. Moreover, it could produce high-grade zinc, lifting Imperial out of the static, low-grade metal market.[4] This smelter design was to receive the Queen's Award for Industry.

The opening of the new plant in June 1968 was the occasion of much rejoicing in Bristol. A special supplement of the *Western Daily Press* bore an advertisement for Imperial showing a happy mother and baby. "It is true," said the caption, "that we have just put into operation the world's largest blast furnace for smelting zinc and lead. And it's a fact that we are the only producer of primary zinc in the country. . . ." But the advertisement went on to boast of certain more homely achievements: "So we help mother to keep her hair in place (father too). And to clean the oven. Then get the right amount of cream on her hands. Repel flies. And freshen the room. And when baby is dowsed in talcum powder or soothed with cream, our zinc is in both products. If he cuts himself we are in the adhesive plaster. . . ."[5]

The guest of honour at the official opening of the new Imperial plant was Harold Wilson, whose premiership at the time was in difficulties. A Director of the Bank of England had just resigned in protest against the Government's economic policies.* A colleague, Richard Crossman, stated that Wilson had "now been made the victim of a daily campaign of character assassination." Even Bristol was angry with Wilson for not providing new docks. On 5 June, the day of Wilson's arrival, the *Western Daily Press* published a carping editorial:

> As Mr. Wilson lunches today amid the splendour and competence achieved by a competitive private industry, he is unlikely to reflect upon the other opportunities lost to the West Country because of the attitude of the Government. . . . For Mr. Wilson has refused . . . to discuss the West Dock, the £15 million lesser alternative to Portbury. . . . Bristol had no industrial hinterland with which to support Portbury, said Mrs. Castle. She favours the clogged chaos of the port approaches of London and Liverpool to the clear motorway from the Midlands to Bristol, the nearest port to New York.[6]

The *Western Daily Press* reporting the ceremony of the opening, was fulsome about Imperial but censorious of Wilson:

> Five hundred guests sitting down to lunch in a large marquee with elaborate lighting fixtures swaying in a boisterous breeze. . . . A special train had brought 120 people from London. They had breakfast on the journey to Bristol and afternoon tea on the trip home. . . . The occasion was the opening of the world's biggest zinc smelter at Avonmouth. . . . As Mr. Wilson spoke at length of the achievements of the Imperial Smelting Company and of the British engineering and metallurgical techniques which led the world, in the background was the faint but insistent hum of a great competitive private industry.

Although Wilson was photographed in protective helmet and overalls, the publicity did not win over Bristol. When he went to catch a London train at Temple Meads station, a small crowd had gathered to boo him. There were shouts of "Resign!", and one shout of "Resign pragmatically!"[7]

The *Western Daily Press* reporter, visiting the Imperial works, had

* This was Cecil King——not Sir Val Duncan, Chairman of RTZ and also a Director of the Bank of England.

detected "the faint but insistent hum of a great competitive private industry." Soon after the opening of the works, Avonmouth residents began to detect a different kind of hum, in the sense of a foul smell, which many attributed to Imperial's towering chimney. Housewives complained that fumes discoloured their washing; people with bronchial conditions complained of pains in the chest; garden plants grew withered or stunted. Air pollution round the industrial estate became so bad that Dr. Robert Hansen, Medical Officer of Health for mid-Gloucestershire, recommended that a plan to build houses in the area should be abandoned, pending a full investigation.[8] The Imperial plant had already begun to trouble the Alkali Inspectorate. This esoteric body originated in 1863 after the first Alkali Act to control the emission of hydrochloric acid gas from the first stage of the Leblanc saltcake process for making alkali or sodium carbonate. The United Kingdom was divided up into five districts in which the Alkali Inspectors went round making tests of the atmosphere and consulting with manufacturers about ways of reducing pollution. The Alkali & Works Regulation Act of 1906 laid down certain statutory standards for the control of emissions; but for most of their works the inspectors followed "presumptive standards", laid down by the Chief Inspector, who can alter them with the development of more efficient methods. The standards deal both with the permitted emission of noxious gases and with means of dispersing them.[9]

The Chief Alkali Inspector's report on Imperial, referring to 1969, said that

> initial results were bad. A major shut-down intervened, but when production and sampling were resumed our worst fears were confirmed. High level meetings were held with the company and plans were laid down for attaining satisfactory conditions. Major modifications are needed and some time will elapse before they can be implemented.

This report was understood to refer to Imperial's number four smelter which had been starting up during this period.

The Imperial works are in an industrial estate which includes other factories that emit smoke or fumes. It is difficult for local people to pin responsibility for the fumes on any one company. This was the experience of Richard Slaughter, the manager of a stud farm at Easter

Compton, three miles from the estate. Early in 1971 he found that some of his newly-born foals were unaccountably going lame:

> After two to three months——just when they started to eat grass for the first time——their joints began to swell and eventually they could barely walk and then only stiff-leggedly. As soon as I sent them away to another farm, eight miles away, they began to get better and are now quite normal. I am convinced there is some kind of metal pollution on the grass.

In bewilderment, Slaughter asked advice from the Ministry of Agriculture, from the National Farmers Union, from the University of Bristol and from an independent neurologist. All of them were agreed that the illness of the foals had been caused by industrial pollution. After giving multi-vitamin injections, Slaughter moved the foals to the Mendips where the animals that were only slightly affected began to recover. Those that were badly affected stayed badly affected. At last Slaughter approached the two major factories on the industrial estate. He said afterwards:

> ICI (Imperial Chemical Industries) were very helpful. . . . The Imperial Smelting Corporation were approached but I'm afraid they didn't seem at all interested. . . . Well, I phoned them——I talked nicely to them and they said they had no comment to make and put the telephone down on me.

On 12 March 1971, the Chairman and Chief Executive of Imperial, Bibbings was questioned about the foals in a BBC West of England TV programme. The interview went:

> Bibbings: I don't know of this case. I don't think I entirely agree with this case. Can you substantiate it?
> BBC: We could, yes.
> Bibbings: Well, will you?
> BBC: Yes, we could easily produce the person who in fact claims that he rang you up.
> Bibbings: Rang me up personally, he said?
> BBC: Rang up. No, rang up Imperial Smelting and in fact had the phone put down on him and then rang ICI who sent someone round to see him.

Bibbings: I find this very difficult to understand [and] accept because we employ an agricultural chemist, we've employed an agricultural chemist now for years and years. He is always available to give advice to local farmers, to local horticulturalists. . . . This is part of the public service provided for years in this district, and I find the accusation very difficult to understand.

BBC: Under what circumstances would your agricultural chemist in fact go out in the field to check possible complaints that were being made?

Bibbings: Well, he is out in the field almost continuously in control of monitoring but he would go out if there was any complaint made to see anybody or . . . to give advice on agricultural matters to anybody that wanted the advice.

BBC: Under what circumstances would Imperial Smelting consider paying compensation?

Bibbings: We have only one circumstance that I know of considered paying compensation, in fact. . . . This was a circumstance of ponies in which there was some doubt as to the origin of the illness of these ponies, and we in fact could not categorically deny that we were responsible for this. We in fact paid compensation in the form of buying the remainder of these ponies; those ponies are still owned by us and still perfectly healthy and happy, if you're able to judge whether a horse is happy or not, and still in the district.

BBC: . . . The Alkali Inspectors were very worried about what was going on here and this was a worry which was expressed in their annual report. . . . Well, I'm curious to know what it was that you were doing here that so perturbed them.

Bibbings: I have no idea what the point is that you're making on this. I'm sorry about this, but I do not know what you're talking about.

BBC: Well, let me quote from the Chief Alkali Inspector's report [here he quoted the extract referred to above]. . . . What I'm asking you is what were the things which first of all caused that concern and secondly what are the major modifications that they thought—

Bibbings: I can only assume that what this is referring to is the start-up of our number four smelter. During the start-up period it is natural that you are inclined to get higher emission than during normal times, but to suggest that we have not co-operated in every possible way. . . .

BBC: Mr. Bibbings, I'm not suggesting that you haven't co-operated with the Alkali Inspectorate, but what I'm interested to know is how much money have you spent as a result of their report, and what have been the results as far as you're concerned in the money you have spent?

Bibbings: Well, specifically we have spent on the number four complex over two million pounds purely on emission control, and the results have certainly brought about quite a considerable reduction in the emission problems there. These are extremely hard to quantify even by an expert in the subject but the results are there and are measurable.[10]

Whatever company is to blame, the Avonmouth industrial estate can be smelt for miles away. Within ten minutes of my getting off the bus, my throat was sore from the airborne fumes. It was worse by the time I had walked to Imperial's main gate, which carries the sign: "CHILDREN AND FEMALE PASSENGERS ARE NOT ALLOWED INSIDE THE WORKS. THIS RULE WILL BE STRICTLY ENFORCED". In the neighbourhood of the smelter, the ditchwater is filmed with bright colours. Few plants can be seen except bindweed, dock and nettles. Thousands of lorries race and roar on the main road north of the Avon.

I called, at random, on 62 St. Andrews Road, which stands on the main road a good half mile from the Imperial Smelter. The owner, R. Bishop, said:

You should have been here this morning. The wife wiped the clothes line and it came away black. She said to me, if it does this to the cloth what's it going to do to your lungs? I've got bronchitis, you see. It's terrible, especially at night when they open the flues. And this is a "residential area". It started to get really bad three years ago.

His wife took up the tale:

The noise from the lorries is terrible. I oughtn't to tell you this, but if it's quiet for a moment I look out to see if there's been an accident. On fine days like this we'd like to leave the windows open but it's impossible. And then there's the flooding. On the industrial estate, they've filled in the reems, the wide ditches, and put in concrete bases, so the water just comes up. It's very low-lying here. When they were digging slit trenches in Avonmouth during the war, they were filling up as soon as you dug them. Our garden's often flooded. Once the Corporation came to inspect the cesspool in one of the gardens near here because they thought it was flooding the garden. But no, the water came from back there, the estate. And now they've put our rates up by £14. . . . Maybe they think we've got a swimming pool in our garden! We used to grow cabbages but now we're afraid to plant anything. If it's not drowned, it turns pink and mauve——you wouldn't believe the wonderful colours. In the last three years it's been really terrible.

She and her husband were speaking to me in autumn 1971, slightly more than three years since the opening of the new plant of the Imperial Smelting Corporation.

The Bishops are a retired couple, who derive no benefit from the Imperial smelter. However, for some Bristol people there were openings for employment at the Imperial plant, even though the new furnace required far fewer men to produce a greater amount of metal. But soon after the opening of its new plant in 1968, Imperial faced financial trouble. The situation worsened until on 22 April 1971 Sir Val Duncan called the zinc smelter "the cross we have to bear".[11] He said that it was running at a loss of £2½ million a year with no immediate chance of recovery. This reflected the world zinc situation rather than the management, which Sir Val said was "as good as anywhere in the world".[12]

The troubles of Imperial could not be blamed on lack of loyalty from the workers. On 8 November 1969, the management presented gold watches, reproduction antique clocks, furniture and radiograms to sixty employees who between them had 2100 years with the Company. On 17 November 1970, a dinner was held at the Grand Hotel, Bristol, for veterans who had served from 25 to 50 years with Imperial. A shop steward, Fred Blake, assured the assembled company:

The first stage of a massive salvage operation has already begun. And I hope this can be followed up with the same determination and resourcefulness that prevailed during two of the most epic salvage operations I remember . . . the Dunkirk evacuation and the return of the *S.S. Great Britain* to Bristol. . . . Then I am sure we will have this company in its rightful place in the forefront of this great industry. I am sure of one thing, however——that is, us old 'uns will not let you down.[13]

The "old 'uns" did not let Imperial down, but on 3 July 1971 the *Bristol Evening Post* reported:

Despair and despondency hit the massive housing estates around Avonmouth today as news of the major smelting works redundancies sunk home. "It will alter our way of life here," said Mr. John O'Brien, one of the 900 workers who had received "you-may-have-to-go" messages. And Mr. Hero Dudbridge, a smelting worker for 47 years, said "I still cannot believe it——I think I am dreaming." His wife Nellie said, "The firm has always been very good, but after all this time it doesn't seem fair." Mr. Len Coleman, who has worked at the works for 39 years, said: "As I am 63 years of age I shall be finished. There is no alternative work here."[14]

In October 1971, RTZ sold its entire Avonmouth zinc smelting and marketing organization to Australian Mining and Smelting, a company formed by a combination of New Broken Hill Consolidated and Conzinc Riotinto Australia, in which RTZ has an 80 percent share. The No. 4 Imperial Smelting Furnace, opened in 1967 by Harold Wilson, now accounted for all Imperial's zinc output. The other furnaces had been closed in July when the 900 men were laid off——and this closure was said to be caused by overproduction. "We just can't sell all we make," the manager lamented. It was explained by RTZ that the sale to the Australians would put mining, smelting and marketing under an integrated command. Some of the Australian shareholders were reportedly less happy with their new ownership of RTZ's "cross".

Meanwhile, Australian Mining and Smelting had taken a 50 percent stake in building a new 50,000 ton-a-year electrolytic zinc smelter in Holland. RTZ's announcement of this smelter did not specify what benefits it would confer on the Bristol unemployed.

*   *   *

In January 1972, when this chapter had been completed and was ready to go to press, the story of the Imperial Smelting Corporation reached a dramatic climax. The issue of *Private Eye* for 28 January (which went on the bookstalls two days before) carried an article headlined "Rio Tinto stinks". "The directors of Rio Tinto Zinc,' it began, "senior trade union officials and the Factory Inspectorate are combining in a desperate attempt to shield the public from the facts about lead poisoning at Rio Tinto's Imperial Smelting Co. smelter in Avonmouth, near Bristol." After recounting earlier instances of anxiety about metallic poisoning, *Private Eye* revealed some recent developments:

> On Monday 6 December, a member of the Amalgamated Union of Engineering Workers sent a medical certificate into the factory excusing him from work because of what his general practitioner described as "lead poisoning". The certificate caused a bit of panic in the factory, and the maintenance shop stewards took the matter up with the management. On 9 December, the 150 maintenance workers staged a token strike in protest against the lack of information about the levels of lead in their blood. The management agreed that the full results of all the tests made up to that time would be made available to a doctor nominated by the unions.

Just before Christmas, the plant was visited by Dr. Bob Murray, the Medical Adviser to the Trades Union Congress, who was shown these results and also took tests himself on about 100 workers. *Private Eye* went on to disclose some of the points from Dr. Murray's report:

> In some parts of the factory, atmospheric tests have shown levels of 76 micrograms per cubic metre. The maximum permissible level is 0·2 mg per cubic metre.
> In the three years since 1968 there have been 20 cases of serious lead poisoning.
> One hundred workers have been suspended from duty on the lead smelting side because of the high lead levels in their blood.

Five hundred workers have recorded lead levels in the blood of 120 micrograms per 100 millimetres... Even the most conservative estimate of the "danger level" is 80 mg per 100 millilitres. On this test, Dr. Murray's own tests on 100 workers showed that 80 were over the danger level.

The *Private Eye* article went on to allege that the company, the local Factories Inspectorate and the local trades unions had all, for various reasons, tried to minimize the dangers of lead fumes in the atmosphere.

Two days after the *Private Eye* article, the daily newspapers reported an eight-week shut-down at the Imperial Smelting Corporation. The story led the front page of the *Guardian* under the headline: "Poison risks close lead smelter plant". The article quoted Dr. Murray as saying that conditions in the factory were the worst he had experienced in 25 years: "There is just no excuse at all for the pollution, and the very real danger to workers in the factory." The British chairman of Rio Tinto, Duncan Dewdney, was quoted as saying that conditions at the complex had been "deplorable . . . and they are still not very good." But the Company was doing everything possible to improve hygiene. "I would not allow any man's health to suffer permanent damage," he said.

NOTES

1. James Savage, *History of Carhampton*, pp. xvii–xx.
2. C. M. MacInnes, *A Gateway of Empire*, p. 336.
3. Meeting attended by author, 6–9–71.
4. *Sunday Times*, 12–2–67.
5. *Western Daily Press*, 10–5–68.
6. *Western Daily Press*, 10–5–68.
7. *Western Daily Press*, 11–5–68.
8. *Sunday Telegraph*, 30–5–71.
9. *Clean Air*, Summer 1971.
10. BBC West of England TV programme, 12–3–71.
11. *Sunday Telegraph*, 20–5–71.
12. *Daily Telegraph*, 22–4–71.
13. *Evening Post*, 17–11–70.
14. *Evening Post*, 3–7–71.

2. ANGLESEY

O potent Minister of Power
What news is this in danger's hour?
Pray, how and when did we create
The Alkali Inspectorate?

I see them—kindly autocrats
With bits of litmus in their hats,
Parading early, testing late,
The Alkali Inspectorate.

The taste of tar is on their tongues,
The breath of hell is on their lungs,
But firm they stand twixt us and fate
The Alkali Inspectorate.
—— By permission of E. S. Turner and *Punch*.

THE Harold Wilson Government was kind to RTZ. We have seen how Wedgwood Benn, the arch-technologist, backed the opening of the uranium mine in South West Africa, a territory held illegally by a cruel and racist regime. We have seen how Wilson himself opened a new plant at the Bristol smelter which was soon to dismiss 900 men and be sold to the Australians. It was again Wilson who encouraged RTZ to build an immense, polluting, and possibly superfluous aluminium smelter in Anglesey——subsidized by a 40 per cent grant out of the taxpayer's pocket. Since the completion of this smelter, which was justified on the grounds that it would bring employment to Anglesey, the unemployment rate on the island has risen to new heights.

Early in 1967, when Britain faced the financial crisis that led to devaluation, the Government decided that Britain must have her own large-scale aluminium industry. For half a century, Britain had depended almost entirely on imports from countries like Canada and Norway with good hydro-electric resources, since power accounts for at least 15 percent of aluminium production costs. It was calculated that Britain, by processing the powdery white alumina (aluminium oxide) instead of importing the aluminium bars, would save as much as £50 million a year on her balance of payments. It was planned to provide the power for these British aluminium plants by building nuclear power stations subsidized by the Government. When the Norwegians, then our partners in EFTA, complained of unfair competition, Anthony Crosland (President of the Board of Trade) assured them: "I firmly believe that our proposals do not carry a risk of any reduction in Norwegian imports to Britain, but will in fact allow an increase."[1]

According to the *Financial Times*, the initiative for the British aluminium plan "came from the mining group Rio Tinto-Zinc, which was interested in an ambitious package involving building and fuelling a nuclear power station linked to a smelter."[2] The alumina supply for the smelter was to come largely from Comalco, the Australian company owned jointly by RTZ and Kaiser. At this time most of Comalco's bauxite from its Weipa reserves went to its own alumina refinery at Gladstone, also in northern Queensland. The alumina was then sent to Comalco's aluminium smelter at Bell Bay in Tasmania. But the Weipa bauxite reserves were so huge and Gladstone had so big a capacity, that RTZ and Kaiser wanted a new smelter in Britain. The cost of freighting alumina from Australia to Britain would be only a tiny item in the cost of the aluminium.

The RTZ plan was hailed by *The Times* as "one of the most imaginative and enlightened industrial projects of the new technological age."[3] Its sister paper the *Sunday Times* was less enthusiastic: "What the Government could have had was a nice clean-cut deal for an aluminium smelter at Holyhead that would have cost the taxpayer heavily and earned a handsome profit for RTZ."[4] At one stage it was suggested that RTZ should buy a half share in the £100 million nuclear power station at Wylfa, also in Anglesey——and then collect 45 percent of the purchase price as an investment grant from the Board of Trade. Unfortunately for RTZ, the other four big manufacturers of aluminium resented this preference for a relative newcomer. They too wanted to set up new aluminium plants backed by investment grants and subsidized electricity. All the contenders wanted to act fast on the assumption, later justified by fact, that a Conservative Government would reduce the investment grants. As a result, not one but three smelter projects were approved—a 100,000 ton plant for British Aluminium at Invergordon; a 60,000 ton plant, to be increased later, for Alcan at Lynemouth, Northumberland; and the one that concerns this chapter, Anglesey Aluminium Corporation, at Holyhead. The Anglesey plant was to be run by RTZ, their old partners Kaiser, and British Insulated Callender's Cables, one of the major aluminium users. Both RTZ and British Aluminium have intimated since that they would not have built the smelters without the benefit of Government grants. Even at the time, the *Economist* complained:

> . . . for the rest of British industry, looking with increasing concern at its power bill, there must be alarm at the philosophy of an electricity supply system created for, industrially speaking, "giants only". True, the DEA [Department of Economic Affairs] has said "in considering projects the Government will have the fullest regard to the competitive position of other firms in the United Kingdom which by their size of location would not have these special contracts available to them". But more than this will be needed if orthodox industrial power consumers are not to feel second-class citizens paying first-class fares.[5]

An RTZ director, Pat Robinson, said afterwards that because his Company had been first in the field it had had "the pick of all the available sites"[6] for a new smelter in Britain. The town of Holyhead has a good deep-water harbour and railway depot. A nuclear power station, which could be used as a source of power, was under construction at Wylfa only a few miles away. Since Anglesey has a chronic unemployment problem, the Labour Government had offered a 40 percent development grant to companies bringing work there. In theory, though not always in practice, the unemployed form a pool of eager, available man-power. With Wylfa power station nearing completion, the construction force could move to Holyhead to work on the site of the smelter.

It has been reported that RTZ made detailed plans for the

Holyhead smelter as early as 1964. "Long before the smelter projects became widely publicized through the Government announcements we were already planning a major development," said Robinson in 1968.[7] In the autumn of 1966, RTZ had started to buy land round Penrhos on the north-east side of Holyhead island.[8] On 3 March 1967, the *Holyhead and Anglesey Mail* published a reader's letter referring to "the possible development near Holyhead" of "the biggest aluminium factory in the world".[9] Later that month the same newspaper published a bunch of letters under the heading of "Holyhead and the Aluminium Rumour". One correspondent complained that

the land that is going to be used for this proposed factory is rich farming land and not so long ago the local authority turned down a request to build a holiday camp on the same site; a request for permission to site some caravans nearby was also turned down by the Welsh Office, yet this filthy, stinking factory (and believe me it will stink) is being pressed for, with no thought of people who have recently built houses nearby which will no doubt lose their value now. Penrhos Beach will become the outfall of the effluence killing all the fish and wild life in the vicinity.[10]

RTZ Services Ltd. issued a soothing statement: "The project may or may not come to fruition . . . it is merely one of a number we are studying". But public argument over the smelter was already fierce.

The main supporters of RTZ were certain councillors and officials of Anglesey County Council, and the District Councils of Holyhead and Valley (the towns on either side of the site). They believed that the smelter would not only bring money and jobs but might attract other industry to the area. *The Times*, as ever friendly to RTZ, reported that the islanders believed themselves near to "an economic miracle". In the eyes of the local authorities, "the Rio Tinto men are the most welcome invaders ever to cross the Menai Straits".[11] The Company had an important supporter in Cledwyn Hughes, the Secretary of State for Wales, who was MP for Anglesey, lived in Holyhead, and had long campaigned for its economic development. The Transport and General Workers Union, which is powerful in Holyhead, favoured the smelter. The district secretary, Idwal Edwards, predicted objections but called on the union to use all its endeavours to ensure that these were put aside.[12] The regional organizer, Tom Jones' described the fight to secure the RTZ plant as "a front line battle in which no effort would be spared".[13] Perhaps TGWU officials felt that the new jobs would be useful in bargaining with the railway and dock authorities who are the main employers in Holyhead. But undoubtedly they had much support from working-class people, as well as from land agents, builders, shop-keepers and publicans. One Anglesey local patriot, W. O. Slade of Llangefni, welcomed the smelter as recompense for an ancient injury to the island. He wrote to the *Holyhead and Anglesey Mail*:

> Anglesey's copper mines were once world-famous and enjoyed the privilege of dictating the world copper price. . . . The Rio Tinto mines in Spain put a stop to all this. They sold cheap copper, and the Anglesey mines could not compete. Parys mines might be an eye-sore to some——to me it's a landmark. I do not know if there is any connection between Rio Tinto Mines and the Smelters. If there is they have a debt to the island which might be still an economic bastion but for the cheap Spanish copper.[14]

Rio Tinto was indeed responsible for the collapse of the Parys mine, whose production of copper fell from 2813 tons in 1872 (the year before the opening of the Rio Tinto mine) to 180 tons only seven years later.[15]

The opposition to RTZ, voiced vehemently in the local press, came from farmers, conservationists, and people with homes near the proposed smelter. The National Farmers Union and the Farmers Union of Wales were perturbed by the proposal to take good arable land for the smelter and for the pylons to bring it power. The farmers were still more perturbed by the possible danger of fluoride effluent. Delegates went to Germany and Switzerland to study the effect of aluminium smelters on local livestock.[16] Professors of botany, zoology and marine biology were consulted and gave their predictions. This possible threat to the atmosphere was the chief concern of those living near the proposed site. Their fears were increased by an article in the *Holyhead and Anglesey Mail* by an Anglesey engineer, Arthur Arnold. Headed "A land-based Torrey-Canyon"——a reference to the tanker that spilled oil off the Cornish coast——the article quoted Gabor and Galbraith to rouse the people of Anglesey from their apathy. Arnold scoffed at the RTZ argument that if the chimney-stack were high there would not be harmful fluoride concentrations:

> Another way of saying this would be: "There would not be high concentration, but it will certainly be spread out." The higher the stack, the more probable it will be that prevailing winds will drive effluent towards Llanddeusant and possibly the new drinking water reservoir in mid-county.... What are property owners in the vicinity to do, and what of Tre-Arddur Bay, which is only 1½ miles away? I would be pleased to contribute to a collection for the erection of a house on Peibio shore for the Prime Minister's use, or even the Welsh Secretary's.[17]

Perhaps unknown to the writer, the Welsh Secretary did actually own a house near the proposed site of the smelter. Most opponents of RTZ conceded that Anglesey needed employment but thought it should come in tourism and light industry. One protestor urged the Government to make Holyhead a container port for overseas goods: "We have non-tidal berthing, railway to hand, and it would make clean use of our splendid harbour."[18] An Anglesey Residents' Association was formed in the summer of 1967. Most of its members were local Welsh, but supporters of RTZ claimed with some justification that its most vocal leaders were middle-class English people who came to the island only for holidays or retirement.

On 4 October 1967, RTZ applied to Anglesey County Council for a site on Holyhead measuring 738 acres, of which 463 would be for industrial purposes and 275 for an "Amenity Area". On 20 October, a group of RTZ executives came to Valley to meet Valley and Holyhead councillors. They brought a scenic model of the site and a pamphlet "Aluminium project for Anglesey", stating that the plant would provide jobs for about 800 people of whom about 200 would be specialists and administrators. Priority would be given to local people in the recruitment of staff. It was emphasized that "there will be no fumes, smell or pollution", although there might be "a plume of water vapour occasionally visible at the top of the ventilation stack". The newspaper report of the meeting included one new, even sensational piece of information:

> There was mention of room on the site to increase the output of

the reduction plant from a first stage of 120,000 tons a year to 300,000 tons. . . . What is more, RTZ plan to import the alumina raw material for the first stage reduction plant, but ultimately they may build another plant to convert crude bauxite into aluminium.[19]

This was news indeed! And it did not escape the attention of one Holyhead resident, N. Ceen, who wrote to the local newspaper next week:

> It has been interesting to follow the way in which public opinion has been so conditioned that even the outrageous demands of Rio Tinto-Zinc's final (phase 2) plan has aroused applause rather than protest. The published production target for phase 2 is 300,000 tons of aluminium per annum to be extracted from bauxite——not the clean white powder originally described. It is well to note that in order to reach that target, 520,000 tons of mud waste would be produced, that 340 million cubic feet of corrosive fluoride gas would be liberated at the anodes and 6,700 million cubic feet of poisonous carbon monoxide and carbon dioxide would be similarly released. . . . Many promises have been made but not one legal guarantee has been given to ensure the purity of our air and the cleanliness of our water supply, our beaches and the sea.

The protest by Ceen against RTZ's "phase 2" plan became so embarrassing that the Company wrote to Anglesey County Council to say it had "no plan or intention to establish such a plant". However, the same letter contained a rather ambiguous reference to the "phase 2" plan. "We have no intention of raising the matter again and would certainly not wish to do so as long as it was apparent that such a plant would not be welcomed by the people of Anglesey."[20]

RTZ played down its "phase 2" plan because it had not yet won over the island to "phase 1". The NFU had dropped its objection to the plan in return for generous compensation, but the FUW turned down the offer and provided a list of 428 objecting island farmers.[21] At least half Anglesey County Council, as well as the officers of its Planning Department, were sceptical of the benefits of a smelter. In an effort to overcome these doubts, RTZ took three councillors and five officials on a free trip to West Virginia to see a smelter run by its

F

partner Kaiser. The party comprised the Chairman, Clerk, Medical
Officer of Health, and the Planning Officer of Anglesey County Council; the Chairman and Clerk of Valley Council; and David Lloyd
Hughes, the Clerk to Holyhead Council (and also the brother of
Cledwyn Hughes, MP and former Cabinet Minister). The Valley Council Clerk Trebor Jones said how much he was looking forward to the
trip——"one like this comes once in a lifetime"[22]——provoking
some waspish comments from the public. "Holyhead Council is possibly already brainwashed into the scheme," wrote Frank Chapman,
a local freelance journalist——"and the delegation to America this
week was little more than a mid-term holiday romp for officials. It
would have been better if they had been joined by just one downright
opponent of the scheme."[23]

The Chairman and Clerk of Anglesey County Council produced a
favourable joint report on Ravenswood, West Virginia. The smelter
had stopped a drift away from the area and had turned a village of
1,100 people into a well-planned, attractive, town of five times the
size. Without exception, everyone interviewed by the delegates welcomed the establishment of the industry, and local farmers reported
no sickness of bones or teeth in their herds. Two churches were now
packed on Sundays where one had sufficed before. But the report had
to admit "that the impact on visual amenity of the Penrhos project
would be much greater than that of the reduction plant at Ravenswood."[24] One should not doubt the honesty of the evidence in
the report, yet it seems odd that these officers of the local authority
should have confined their research to a foreign smelter chosen by
one of the applicants, run by another, on a trip paid for by both.

The Anglesey Medical Officer of Health had reservations about the
Ravenswood smelter. He went to some pains to stress that he did *not*
see a bauxite plant in Virginia, yet he included in his report a photo-
graph of "a modern Bauxite Plant——for which planning approval is
not sought at this time but which development is not discounted
in the brochure submitted by RTZ." In other words, he was pointing
out that the Ravenswood Plant offered no evidence of the effects
should RTZ introduce "phase 2". Moreover, he was uneasy about the
fluoride emission at Ravenswood. Ont of the Kaiser senior executives
at Ravenswood had told the MOH "that if he were building a plant
for the Government and not for a private concern, he would insist on

the activated alumina treatment in baghouses together with a tall
stack——the stack being a safety valve in case of baghouse break-
down". The MOH noted that the level of fluoride emission at Ravenswood was 16·5 percent above what it had been when the plant
started. The technologists were ignorant of the cause, which could
not be attributed to increased production of aluminium.[25]

On 14 November 1967, Anglesey County Council met to debate
RTZ's application to build a smelter on Holyhead. One white-haired
old man gave an impassioned speech in Welsh, to the bewilderment of the RTZ executives who had been asked to the meeting.
Other councillors asked, in English, if it was right for Anglesey to
sell its birthright for a mess of pottage. As a result the council
decided to seek expert advice from university sources before voting
in one month's time. When this decision was taken the Clerk to the
ACC threw down his pen in an angry gesture. He was an eager advocate of the RTZ plan, and during the next month he summoned,
individually, every member of the Council for a persuasive talk on the
need for a smelter.[26] However, university professors who had been
called in by the Council warned of the dangers of atmospheric pollution unless RTZ took the most stringent preventative measures.
When the smelter came up once more in debate on 14 December, the
Planning Committee of Anglesey County Council tied 10:10 on
whether to grant the RTZ application. The Chairman used his casting
vote in favour of RTZ but later withdrew his decision. The full Council meeting that afternoon was overwhelmingly favourable to the
application, but opposition from farmers and other groups was still
so strong that the Clerk and Chairman decided to ask the Secretary
of State for Wales for a Public Inquiry.

The Public Inquiry opened at Holyhead on 9 January 1968. The
opposition to RTZ came from the Anglesey Residents' Association,
the two farmers unions, and the Council for the Protection of Rural
Wales. Early on in the proceedings, the National Farmers Union withdrew its opposition in return for compensation. The Counsel for RTZ,
Keith Goodfellow QC, appealed to national as well as to local patriotism by arguing that the plant was important to Britain.[27] Two
scientists employed by Kaiser were brought from the United States to
deny "that there would be any noise, smell or air pollution from
the proposed plant".[28] A barrister for Anglesey County Council

condemned the "so-called Anglesey Residents' Association", and claimed support for the plant from the overwhelming majority of the people of the island. The planning consultants for RTZ advanced the curious notion that the smelter chimney would somehow improve the landscape.

The lucid report by County Planning Officer N. Squire Johnson, presented in November 1967, gave a summary of the arguments for and against the smelter. The possible disadvantages he envisaged included the ugliness of overhead power lines that might be erected to serve the smelter and the possible introduction of a bauxite plant and other heavy industry, as well as the other dangers which have already been discussed. But the subject that was to dominate the three-week Inquiry was the danger of fluoride emission from the smelter chimney. In his report, the County Planning Officer referred to the claim in the RTZ pamphlet that "a well-designed modern aluminium plant does not emit smells or fumes, which could cause harm". But he remarked that

> the experience which Anglesey residents have had in connection with similar installations has not been too happy. The OCTEL plant at Amlwch, which the planning authority were assured would not cause any nuisance, under certain weather conditions is anything but pleasant, and the Ferodo factory built outside Portdinorwic is a source of the most unpleasant smells for many periods during the year. There is no doubt that the RTZ Company were being as honest as they can when they say that the plant would not have any smell or fumes which could cause harm, but similar assurances have been given before, and under certain conditions smells and fumes have been emitted. There is also the possibility of something going wrong with a plant of this complexity.[29]

Similar warnings were given by the Medical Officer of Health. After enumerating the hazards of a smelter like the one at Ravenswood, the MOH declared: "I am confident that if *all* modern methods of treatment of such gaseous effluents are incorporated in modern plants (i.e. activated alumina baghouses and tall stacks) using modern techniques of production that this hazard to agriculture can be eliminated." The Ministry of Health and the Alkali Inspectorate of the Ministry of Housing and Local Government had confirmed that "no health hazard to humans or farm animals can be expected". The MOH went on to report:

> The Alkali Inspectorate, I understand, have from the outset been consulted by RTZ's chemical engineering consultants about pollution problems and their proposals for solving them. Mr. Ireland, the Chief Alkali Inspector, said that they have found the Company most co-operative in the control of its air pollution at other sites. I understand from one of the Company's Medical Officers that it is their intention, should approval for building be given, that an industrial medical service to look after the health of the workers be set up and that monitoring of levels of noxious substances within and without the plant be made operational immediately and I hope beforehand.

However, the MOH pointed out that the aluminium industry included four different kinds of production: the mining of bauxite and its conversion to alumina; the electrolytic reduction of alumina to aluminium; alloying or fabrication; and the harnessing of by-products from the above products. He concluded his report with this important warning:

> Since each of these processes present different and important aesthetic, planning, social and health considerations, I think it essential that we obtain assurances from the Company as to their intentions regarding the future development of their interests in Holyhead should this scheme receive approval by the necessary Authorities, before the County Council gives its blessing to this proposed factory——if we do not, we could well be caught in an avalanche with no return to the status quo.[30]

At the Inquiry, RTZ offered oral assurances but no legal guarantees about future plans for the Holyhead works, including the hypothetical "phase 2" treatment of bauxite. Even more important, RTZ gave no legally binding guarantees on the level of fluoride emission from the aluminium smelter. When the Inquiry opened, Anglesey County Council stipulated that the fluorine content of the gases emitted from the pot rooms should not exceed 360 lb/day with fluorine concentration not exceeding 0.5 mg/m^3 and that the fluorine content of the gases from the stack should not exceed 330 lb/day with fluorine concentration not exceeding 2·5 mg/m³. The Council also proposed that the low-level emission of gases from the pot rooms should be scrubbed. The Company rejected this proposal as "impracticable". RTZ insisted that the works would need to emit only 284 lb/day of fluorine at 0·44 mg/m³ from the pot rooms, and only 270 lb/day of fluorine at 2·2 mg/m³ from the stack. When RTZ gave this estimate of emissions well below the maximum set by the County Council, the listeners at the Inquiry did not trouble to press RTZ for legal guarantees. They were still more reassured when a letter was read from the Alkali Inspectorate expressing profound satisfaction with the measures RTZ had prepared to control the effluents. It was felt that the problem of air pollution could now be left to the Alkali Inspectorate. The Inquiry petered out, and the Inspector recommended the smelter. As regards air pollution:

> Leaving aside fluorine, he [the Inspector] is satisfied that dispersed emissions would have no adverse effects either upon human health or upon the environment at large. As regards fluoride emissions, he accepts the calculated estimates of the Company as representing a reasonable assessment of what might ultimately eventuate, but nevertheless considers it right to have regard to an uncertainty factor of 2, in order to provide for imponderables, especially the achieved levels of potroom containment and the vagaries of dispersion in ever-changing meteorological conditions. On the basis of the Company's estimates, or even applying the uncertainty factor of 2, the Inspector concludes that there are no reasonable grounds for expecting any hazard to human health, either within or beyond the limits of the site, or for assuming that the general environment would be significantly affected.[31]

When the smelter was built and went into production, the levels of pollution soon exceeded those that RTZ had predicted. With the permission of the Alkali Inspectorate, total emissions were up 54·7 percent above the stated level, while emissions of fluoride from the main stack were three times greater than the amount that Anglesey County Council had laid down as tolerable. It was officially explained that since the Inquiry, RTZ had designed a different kind of smelter.

Originally there were to have been two stacks——one of 300 ft. and one (for the anode plant) of 125 feet. But in practice all emissions (except some from the potroom louvres) went through a single stack of 400 feet. There were also reports that the fluoride extraction plant was giving trouble and had broken down twice. Duncan Dewdney, Chairman of Anglesey Aluminium Ltd. and Executive Director of RTZ, was asked what he would do if the Company could not contain pollution at the new level of 86 percent as against the previous 95 percent. According to *The Ecologist* magazine,

> He replied that the Company would have to spend more on scrubbing equipment. Why then, he was asked, were the Company not prepared to install equipment that would maintain a scrubbing efficiency of 95 percent as promised, particularly since the smelter had been constructed under its budgeted cost. It appears that the Company has no intention of either installing this equipment or of going back to the original figures.[32]

It is important to bear in mind that air pollution from factories can normally be prevented if sufficient money is spent. At any rate, that is the view of F. E. Ireland, the Chief Alkali Inspector, who said in a lecture in Manchester in November 1970:

> If money were unlimited, there would be very few if any problems of air pollution control which could not be solved fairly quickly. We have the technical knowledge to absorb gases, arrest grit, dust and fumes, and prevent smoke formation. The only reason why we still permit the escape of these pollutants is because economics are an important part of the word "practicable". Most of our problems are cheque book rather than technical, and attitudes which take little account of the economics of scarce resources, on which there are so many claims, can so easily blur the importance of the right choice of priorities.[33]

This lecture was given on 10 November. On 3 November Inspector Ireland had replied to a letter from Mrs. M. Biggs of Trearddur Bay, Holyhead, who had complained of the air pollution from Anglesey Aluminium. He wrote in this letter:

> We do not accept that the estimates submitted by the Company

at the Public Inquiry were binding in any way. They were given in all good faith as typical of what emissions were expected in order to meet our targets, *on which the figures were based* [italics added]. They represented our preliminary estimate of what might be achieved on the evidence of known technology. The important point of the Inquiry, in relation to air pollution, was that the Company should meet the requirements of the Alkali Inspectorate. When we got down to details of design and in the light of practical tests carried out in the USA on full-scale plant, it soon became obvious that we had to change our original thoughts on prevention and dispersion in order to keep the project viable. . . . Industry cannot be handicapped by rigid rules based on estimates.

To which one can only reply "Why not?" The point of the Public Inquiry was not, as Ireland seems to believe to help RTZ to make money out of its smelter, but to safeguard the interests of the people of Anglesey. In the same letter, Ireland rebukes Mrs. Biggs:

The important point, which you seem to miss, is that it is the effect of the emissions at ground-level which matters most and not the mass emission of pollutants. In this, our requirements have not changed and the environment is safeguarded just as much under the new conditions as under the old, perhaps even with a minor improvement.[34]

Another important point which Ireland seems to miss is that the *mass* emission of pollutants is just as harmful when they are widely scattered as when they descend on a patch round the factory.

Nevertheless there is evidence of pollution close to the plant. Since the prevailing wind in Holyhead comes from the south-west, the area most affected is along the shore to the north. The 275-acre tract of company land set aside as a so-called "Amenity Area" is skirted by what the Company calls "a nature trail". A pamphlet, put out by RTZ, reads: "Welcome to Penrhos Nature Trail. The path you are about to follow is a new one laid down by Anglesey Aluminium Ltd. and forms the course of a nature trail established by the Company in response to European Conservation Year." Also laid down by Anglesey Aluminium Ltd. is a fine film of dust which, as I saw in autumn 1971, turned blackberries pale white.

One of the people living near Anglesey Aluminium's "Nature Trail" is Douglas Bond of 2 Brunyglos, who told me:

> We don't grow anything in the garden now. It would turn strange colours and we wouldn't feel like eating it. If you take the dog for a walk he comes back all black. . . . We got used to the vibration. We didn't mind it so much as the flying dust. There's a drain going out from the works to the sea. It's supposed to be only surface water but they throw in oil and things. . . . There used to be a fieldful of mushrooms and cows but not now. Nobody from the firm has been here to see if we're all right.

His wife wiped a rag on the washing line and showed me the streak of dirt. "Last week it was terrible," she went on. "But when it blows from the north we have a washing-day like nobody's business——bedspreads and all. . . . You get a sulphury taste in the mouth. . . . All the pheasants and birds have disappeared."[35] Among those who lived at Penrhos, near to the smelter, was Cledwyn Hughes, the MP and Cabinet Minister. He has since moved to Trearddur Bay on the other side of Holyhead Island.[36]

The main argument put forward for the establishment of a smelter was the extra jobs it would bring to Anglesey. Certainly by late 1971 there were some 800 people employed by Anglesey Aluminium. Many of these were local people. For example, the Clerk of Holyhead Urban District Council, David Lloyd Hughes (the brother of Cledwyn Hughes MP), announced in November 1968 that he was going to become the Administrative Manager to Anglesey Aluminium Company. He took with him as his assistant the former Assistant Clerk of the Council, Miss D. M. Williams, who had also collaborated with Hughes on a book entitled "Holyhead: The Story of a Port".[37] Even former critics of the company later took employment with it. On the other hand, some former friends of the Company afterwards turned into opponents. One of the foremost is Tom Jones, the Transport and General Workers' Union leader, who had fought a "front line battle" for the smelter, only to see it declared a "one-union shop" for the Electrical and Plumbing Trades Union. Jones described this decision as a "stab in the back".[38]

Before the smelter, unemployment in Anglesey averaged 7 or 8 percent, although it had risen as high as 12·5 percent. During the period of construction, when there were ample labouring jobs, unemployment fell to 4·8 percent. As the construction work tailed off, unemployment increased to 11·6 percent in October 1971. The area manager for the Department of Employment, R. K. Lewis, predicted that unemployment was bound to go over 12 percent in the winter.[39] In the Holyhead region alone there were 446 men and 84 women unemployed. The Deputy Planning Officer for Anglesey, Mr. Powell, said that industrial projects on the island caused a new problem when the construction died away:

> A chap comes over from Ireland, say, and he gets married and his children are doing their "O" levels and he doesn't feel like moving again. It's the same with our own young men. They would have left the island but they stayed for the construction work and when that dies away it's too late for them to move. Unemployment used to be round 6–8 percent but now it's over 10 percent which is completely unacceptable.[40]

This experience of new projects helps to explain why the County Planning Department fought the plan (approved by its Council) to build an oil terminal for Shell on the north of the island.

The smelter has so far been discussed in relation only to Anglesey and the little district of Holyhead. The arguments about jobs or beauty, although important, could be described as parochial. One should also take a look at the smelter in terms of its national, even international meaning. As we have heard, RTZ might not have built a smelter in Britain without a substantial Government grant. The Government of the time defended such grants by the necessity to strengthen Britain's balance of payments. Whether such measures were necessary I leave to the economists. One can only point out that shortly after the Anglesey smelter had been approved, Labour Chancellor Roy Jenkins revealed to an astonished country that, due to an accounting error, Britain's reported deficit over the last few years had in fact been a substantial surplus. Yet for the sake of our balance of payments, Britain had spent colossal sums on private-enterprise industries——such as Rolls-Royce, the Concorde project and Upper Clyde Shipbuilders——which now appear to have been economically unprofitable.

Britain's decision to build three new aluminium smelters has since been deplored by important men in the industry. Delegates to a meeting of the Organization of European Aluminium Smelters (held in London in September 1971) were told by Stewart Spector, chief analyst of Oppenheimer & Co., that production would have to be kept in check if the excess world capacity were to be brought into balance. He said that programmes to introduce new smelters in 1972 "most definitely will have to be postponed, cancelled or kept idle upon completion". He said that to obtain a 9 percent return on investment capital on a new smelter a primary ingot price of 31 cents per pound was needed against today's market price level of 24 cents per pound.

At the same meeting, Krome George, the president of Aluminium Co. of America (the world's largest producer of aluminium), blamed British policy for adding new capacity to the world market. He told the delegates:

> Here in the United Kingdom a major primary aluminium indus-
> try has been created literally overnight, based I must say in all
> candour, on Government construction grants of up to 40 percent
> and on Government-subsidized [electric] power. It has disturbed
> well-established market relations——particularly in Norway and
> Canada and through Canada to the United States——and for what
> purpose? I assume some Government planning objective was
> achieved; but our industry has been damaged simply because
> excess capacity was created which would not have been created if
> normal economic and financial restraints had been allowed to op-
> erate. As a result many private investors in the aluminium industry
> around the world stand to suffer financially in one way or the
> other.[41]

It should be said in fairness here that if the Anglesey smelter was a mistake, the blame rests *not* with RTZ but with the politicians, in Anglesey and in London, who encouraged its construction. RTZ is not responsible to the British Government or to the people of Anglesey. It is responsible to its shareholders in Britain and abroad. And here one must stop to consider, briefly, the effect of the Anglesey smelter on Comalco.

Comalco's Weipa deposit provides the bauxite for its alumina plant at Gladstone, also in Queensland. Much of this alumina is now shipped for smelting to Holyhead. It will be recalled that the Weipa deposit was let by the Queensland Government to Comalco for a peppercorn rent. Furthermore, the processing of bauxite to alumina is not a very profitable operation. The profitable part of the operation, smelting aluminium from alumina, is done in Tasmania, Holyhead, or other smelters abroad. Those Australians who purchased Comalco shares in the famous floatation of 1970 might ponder two questions:

Did RTZ, in 1967, consider building a new smelter in Queensland? In the past this would have been unthinkable, since Queensland lacks the hydro-electric resources on which smelting used to depend. But by 1967, RTZ was looking to nuclear power as a substitute and indeed had offered to build a nuclear power station to fuel its Anglesey smelter. The Australian Government at about this time was expressing the wish to build an Australian nuclear power industry. The uranium was available——from RTZ's own Mary Kathleen mine, which had been closed when RTZ switched the flow of production from Australia to its Canadian subsidiaries.

The second question leads on from the first. With the opening of the Anglesey Aluminium works, RTZ (with its partners Kaiser) now operates smelters in both the UK and Australia. It can control the flow of aluminium according to demand, just as it also controls much of the flow of uranium on three continents (and perhaps soon on a fourth). This international control puts Comalco into the same position as Mary Kathleen Uranium. As the Australian subsidiary of a foreign company, it is vulnerable to a depression in the price of aluminium. If RTZ, a British company which has received a 40 percent construction grant to build a smelter in Britain, had to reduce production either in Anglesey or in Tasmania, which would it choose? It is a question that might well be asked by Comalco shareholders.

Notes

1. *Liverpool Daily Post*, 11–5–68.
2. *Financial Times*, 6–10–71.
3. *Times*, 26–5–67.
4. *Sunday Times*, 8–10–67.
5. *Economist*, 7–10–67.
6. *Times*, 25–7–68.

7. *Times*, 25–7–68.
8. *Ecologist*, June 1971. Article by Richard Thompson Coon, a marine biologist.
9. *Holyhead and Anglesey Mail*, 31–3–67.
10. *Holyhead and Anglesey Mail*, 31–3–67.
11. *Times*, 12–8–68. See also *Liverpool Daily Post* 18–10–67 in an article headed "Rio Tinto Zinc gives hint to local councillors. Giant Valley project may be only a start."
12. *Holyhead and Anglesey Mail*, 11–6–67.
13. *Holyhead and Anglesey Mail*, 8–12–67.
14. *Holyhead and Anglesey Mail*, 24–11–67.
15. Robert Hunt, *British Mining* (London 1887), p. 897.
16. *Ecologist*, June 1971.
17. *Holyhead and Anglesey Mail*, 20–10–67.
18. *Holyhead and Anglesey Mail*, 7–7–67.
19. *Liverpool Daily Post*, 18–10–67.
20. *Holyhead and Anglesey Mail*, 27–10–67.
21. *Ecologist*, June 1971.
22. *Holyhead and Anglesey Mail*, 27–10–67.
23. *Holyhead and Anglesey Mail*, 3–11–67.
24. County of Anglesey. Report by Chairman and Clerk (Enclosure B). 9–11–67.
25. County of Anglesey. Report by County Medical Officer (Enclosure D).
26. *Ecologist*, June 1971.
27. Transcript of Inquest held in Holyhead. January 1968.
28. Transcript of Inquest held in Holyhead. January 1968.
29. County of Anglesey. Report by County Planning Officer (Enclosure C).
30. County of Anglesey. Report by County Medical Officer. (Enclosure D).
31. Letter from D. J. Tallis, Welsh Office, Cardiff, conveying approval for Rio Tinto-Zinc's application. 27–6–68.
32. *Ecologist*, June 1971.
33. *Clean Air*, Summer 1971.
34. Letter from F. E. Ireland, Chief Alkali Inspector, Ministry of Housing and Local Government to Mrs. M. I. Biggs, Seavale Cottage, Ton-y-capel Road, Trearddur Bay, Holyhead, Anglesey. 3–11–70.
35. Interview with author. October 1971.
36. *Sunday Times*, 5–9–71.
37. *Holyhead and Anglesey Mail*, 8–11–68.
38. *Financial Times*, 6–10–71.
39. Interview with author. November 1971.
40. Interview with author. October 1971.
41. *Times*, 11–9–71.

3. MERIONETH

The Latin adjective ob-scenus ("unlucky" or "inauspicious") took its present sense of obscene from the presentation on what had been a wholly religious scene (scaena) of words and acts that would offend and be punished by local deities. The Rio Tinto-Zinc Company . . . is now bent on industrializing a peculiarly sacred district in Gwynedd.
——Robert Graves on RTZ's mining prospects in North Wales. Letter in *Western Daily Mail*, 12 December 1970.

As individuals we are no less enthusiastic than any other nature lovers and we are examining in great detail what steps could be taken to ensure that any mining activities which might take place in this particular corner of the National Park should not disturb the ecology or the reasonable enjoyment of those who visit this beautiful area for recreational purposes.
——Sir Val Duncan, Chairman of RTZ, at the Annual General Meeting on 19 May 1971.

A Bill introduced in the Commons today enables the Government to contribute 35 percent of the cost of exploring for and evaluating mineral deposits in Britain and on the Continental Shelf.
——Press Association report, 11 November 1971.

Our environment is created by thousands of individual decisions, some small, some great.
——Prime Minister Edward Heath, quoted in *The Times*, 28 October 1971.

Turning from the general to the particular, the Duke [of Edinburgh] made it clear that he detects some change in popular attitudes. Without naming the companies concerned [BP and

Rio Tinto-Zinc] he said he believed that possible drilling for oil
in the New Forest and mining for minerals in a Welsh beauty
spot would have created no argument 50 years ago. Now there
will be a hell of an argument. Well, this is quite an advance.
——*The Times*, 6 September 1971.

At home my Government's first care will be to increase employment. . . . Legislation will be brought before you . . . for assisting
the exploration of our mineral resources.
——From Her Majesty's Most Gracious Speech to both Houses
of Parliament, delivered on Tuesday 2 November 1971.

LIKE most mining companies, RTZ is shy of publicity. In southern
Africa, and above all South West Africa, it operates in something like
secrecy. In Australia it is disguised behind its subsidiaries. The name
Rio Tinto-Zinc does not appear in Anglesey Aluminium or in Bristol's
Imperial Smelting Corporation. The recent and doubtless unwelcome
fame of RTZ derives from its plans to prospect for minerals in Snowdonia. Since then the Company has been hotly discussed in Parliament and in the national press; Sir Val Duncan and other directors
have stated their case on TV; the conservation movement, which
grew strong in Britain during the 1960s, has made RTZ a target of
protest. Celebrities such as the Duke of Edinburgh and the poet
Robert Graves have joined the debate on RTZ, proving the truth of
Sir Val Duncan's maxim that "Taking the wealth out of the soil is an
emotional business and it is only too easy for political and nationalistic feelings to run high." Yet mining for metals in Britain is not
new.

British children's history books begin with the white-robed
Phoenicians who came to Cornwall to buy our tin. Later the Romans
mined British tin, lead, copper and gold. Until the second half of the
nineteenth century, England and Wales were the world's largest producers of tin and copper, but precious metals like silver and gold were
the property of the Crown and therefore did not attract legitimate
miners. As late as 1796, soldiers were called in to expel hundreds of
Irish peasants who were washing for gold in a stream in County Wick-
low. By the end of the nineteenth century, Britain's mining industry

had been ruined by competition from Spain, Chile, Bolivia, Australia and South Africa, not reviving again until the 1960s when the war in Vietnam caused a jump in the world price of metals. Cornish tin mines were reopened and now produce one-fifth of the country's needs for this metal. In Anglesey, in 1967, the locals said almost with disbelief that "if the price of copper goes any higher they'll want to re-open the Parys mine." The price went higher, and sure enough, a North American company came to study the mine. Paradoxically, by the time that most of these companies had passed the prospecting stage, the world price of metals had dropped by as much as a third; Britain's consumption of copper fell 5 percent in 1970 alone. Nevertheless, the mining companies have continued prospecting on the assumption that metal prices will pick up again. Moreover, modern mining processes make it profitable to work low-grade deposits that once were considered uneconomic. Great earthmovers and dragline excavators can tear away mountains to make open-cast mines of several miles in diameter and half a mile in depth. It is just this fact that most worries conservationists.

A map of the British mineral rush shows prospectors, literally, from Land's End to John O'Groats. Often the men on the drill rigs refuse to name the company that employs them; indeed they may not know it, since most big mining houses use a sub-contractor for exploration work. However RTZ is known to have looked for or to be looking for copper, nickel, chromium, and gold in Ulster, the Shetland Islands, many sites on the mainland of Scotland, the Isle of Man, the Lake District and North Wales.[1] Since metallic minerals are most often found in older rocks, which in turn are found in upland Britain, these sites are almost confined to the western part of the kingdom. Unhappily, they are often found in hills, mountains and moorland of striking natural beauty. RTZ's prospecting site in Northern Ireland includes the Mountains of Mourne, which are not only beautiful but also of sentimental importance to the embattled Ulster Catholics.[2] The fact that the exploration licence was given to RTZ, an English company, by the Protestant Stormont Government could cause trouble if mining begins.

Mines and quarries may soon be dug in the ten upland areas which were created National Parks in 1949. Prospecting is going on for tin on Dartmoor, limestone in the Brecon Beacons, fluorspar in the Peak

District, various rocks in Northumberland and the Peak District,
potash on the North York Moors, and non-ferrous metals in the Lake
District. But public concern has centred on Snowdonia, in North
Wales, which many British people (this author included) consider
the loveliest region of these islands. The preface to William Condry's
splendid new book calls Snowdonia "something quite peculiar and
special——a haven of biologists, archaeologists, palaeontologists,
topographers, geologists, historians and climbers that has no parallel
in the world".[3]

Supporters of RTZ sometimes imply that the conservationists want
Snowdonia to be wild, uninhabited and sterile. This is to mis-
understand what nature-lovers mean by nature. They wish Snowdonia not to become sterile but to remain fruitful. The ancient axes
and arrowheads found everywhere in Snowdonia prove that man has
long been living and working there. For centuries, man-made fields,
hedgerows, paths, roads, bridges and villages have patterned the
landscape. Livestock, poultry and domestic animals have for
centuries shared the pastures with wild beasts and birds. The ravens,
which kill young lambs and peck out the eyes of living sheep, are
ancient enemies of the local farmers——farmers whose way of life is
an essential element of Britain's human diversity.

Snowdonia is a haven not from man, but from industrial man. It
has been largely free until now from the noise, dirt, ugliness, and
atmospheric pollution of nearby Merseyside, south-east Lancashire
and the Black Country. The use of pesticides has caused some
damage; the roads are thronged with lorries and cars; and Snowdonia, thanks to the RAF, has more than its share of low-flying jets.
Nevertheless it remains a naturalist's paradise. The polecat can still
be seen there; the rivers are famous for sea-trout and salmon, if not
in such quantities as when Fluellen boasted in Shakespeare's Henry
IV; buzzards are numerous, the peregrine falcon is quite common,
and even the merlin is still sometimes seen on a rocky, heathery
mountainside.

The cult of Snowdonia's beauty began during the 1770s and
reached its peak during the 1790s. It has been calculated that in that
decade, when England was at war with France and the Grand Tour of
the Continent was therefore impracticable, a tourist book on Snowdonia was published every six months. Romantic writers were awed

G

by the mountain crags and cataracts. Wordsworth was one of the many who climbed Snowdon by moonlight, but one of the few to write a worthy account of it. Both Coleridge and De Quincy came on walking tours. Shelley lived for a while at Tremadoc, near the present artistic colony of Penrhyndeudraeth. The English writer Thomas Love Peacock was even more passionate in his love for Snowdonia than the Welshman George Borrow, who wrote *Wild Wales*.

The beauties of Wales draw ever more tourists. Holidaymakers spent £108 million in Wales in 1970, or 15 per cent above the previous record in the year of the investiture of Prince Charles. It has been calculated that Wales earns more per person from tourists than any country in the world except Austria and Switzerland. The proportion would be higher by far if one took only North Wales, where the population is small but the tourist attractions enormous. Many holidaymakers go straight to the North Wales seaside resorts like Rhyl. Llandudno and Barmouth; but inland Snowdonia draws hundreds of thousands of walkers and mountaineers. In 1970, the tourist information centre at Betws-y-Coed, inside the National Park, received 40,000 visitors, of whom a quarter came from overseas. The Chairman of the Wales Tourist Board, T. Mervyn Jones, said that tourist revenue was of growing benefit to remote inland areas. He went on:

> Here tourism has come, and in our view must only come, to fulfil, and never destroy, the prime base industry of agriculture. We plan for tourism and its revenue to supplement farm revenue and so make possible the extension of farming. A flourishing agriculture is the greatest tourist attraction; decay its repulsion.[4]

It is important to stress the economic benefits that tourism brings to North Wales, since many North Welshmen and supporters of RTZ, say that the tourists come for only a few months of the year and do not spend much money. National feeling stokes the resentment. In Merioneth, where RTZ is prospecting, one hears more Welsh than English spoken in shops, buses or pubs. Here, as in Anglesey, there is strong local prejudice against English people who make their money in Birmingham or Manchester and take a house in Wales for the weekends or their retirement. The inflow of English people is matched by an outflow of young Welsh men and women, who find no scope for their talents at home and therefore go to work in England. Although North Wales is growing in population, the increase is mostly in large north coast towns, like Bangor, and in Anglesey, where industrial development has increased both the population and the unemployment. Depopulation is most marked in Merioneth, most of which is within the National Park. Understandably, though I believe unreasonably, some Merioneth people blame the National Park for depopulation.

There have been many attempts in this century to bring jobs and industry to Snowdonia. Since the 1920s the Forestry Commission has changed the landscape of much of Snowdonia by planting forests of conifers. Local people complain that employees of the Commission have little opportunity for advancement, while the processing of the timber is done in England. Lovers of natural beauty complained that dark, rectangular pine forests spoil the contours and colour-scheme of Snowdonia. The *Daily Telegraph* columnist "Peter Simple", who is not a man of the Left, has been moved to describe the Forestry Commission as an example of "English Imperialism".[5]

The threat posed by industry to the beauty of Snowdonia is exemplified by the nuclear power station at Trawsfynydd, near Ffestiniog. This great grey edifice and the column of giant pylons which it feeds have desecrated one of the loveliest parts of Snowdonia. Further north, at Blaenau Ffestiniog, one can see the vestiges of the slate quarrying industry which flourished for most of the nineteenth century. A few score men are still at work, but slate tiles for roofing have long been priced out of the mass market by other materials. The physical mess left by abandoned quarries is so unsightly that Blaenau Ffestiniog had to be left out of the National Park of which it forms the geographical centre. There were rumours, late in 1971, that the industry might be due for revival, thanks to the fashion for slate among architects and interior decorators.

Supporters of RTZ point out that Snowdonia has for centuries had metal mines. Archaeologists date the first use of bronze, an alloy of copper and tin, to at least 2000 years before the Roman invasion. Since there is no tin in Snowdonia, the bronze weapons and instruments which have been found there were probably brought from outside. The Romans whose principal mines were at Rio Tinto in Spain, took an interest in Snowdonia. As William Condry says:

Two copper cakes, stamped in Latin, have been found at the foot of Carnedd Llywelyn. It seems reasonable to suppose that both copper- and lead-mines existed in Snowdonia prior to Roman times and that it was these mines which most attracted the Romans to North Wales. Copper-mines, like other metal-mines in Snowdonia, have always been rather small and scattered because the ore-lodes vary much in richness and are very irregularly and uncertainly distributed in both the Cambrian and Ordovician sedimentary rocks, into which the minerals were precipitated from solutions ascending from the lower heated layers of the earth's crust.[6]

These small and scattered ore-lodes would not present a problem to modern companies mining with open-cast methods.

In West Merioneth, where RTZ is exploring, the copper belt coincides with the gold belt and many mines have been worked for both metals. The belt extends from Bontddu (on the Mawddach Estuary), eastwards and upstream to Rhobell Fawr, where, according to the *Topical Dictionary of Wales* published in 1833, there were "vast quantities of copper". The author recounts how

A gentleman resident in Dolgelly [Dolgellau], learning that peat from Dolfrwynog in the parish of Llanfachreth was useless as a manure, had it analysed and found it contained copper. So he had a great quantity of peat cut and burned in kilns and shipped the ashes to Swansea where they were made to yield excellent copper. From this circumstance it has been supposed that the surrounding mountains teem with copper ore which, through the medium of springs, has impregnated the peat of the hollows below with a solution of sulphate of copper.[7]

RTZ has explored two separate sites in this gold and copper region of West Merioneth. The first, the Mawddach Estuary between the railway bridge in the south-west and Penmaenpool Bridge in the north-east, covers a 1775-acre area about five miles long and between $\frac{1}{4}$ and $1\frac{1}{4}$ miles in width. RTZ's plan reportedly involved dredging the area with one or more dredgers of $320 \times 80 \times 80$ feet in size. Such a vessel would have to be floated either by digging out a lagoon or by flooding the estuary with a barrage near the existing railway station. The second RTZ site covers 2475 acres round Capel Hermon, a village scattered through the south-east part of the Coed-y-Brenin forest about four miles north of Dolgellau (the county town). Here the search was and is for copper. If ore is found of sufficient grade and quantity, RTZ would want to employ opencast mining with perhaps two to four pits, each about 200 acres in area and hundreds of feet deep. The life of the mine would be from 15 to 30 years, requiring initial investment of well over £40 million. Let us take a closer look at the areas of the two sites.

The view south over the Mawddach Estuary to the mountain Cader Idris is among the most lovely in Europe. John Ruskin once wrote: "There is but one finer walk in Europe than the walk from Dolgellau to Barmouth, and that is the walk from Barmouth to Dolgellau." Nor is its value scenic only. Among its delights to naturalists is a stretch of bog near Arthog, whose vegetation includes the St. John's wort and the greater spearwort, and whose birds include the sedge warbler, grasshopper warbler, reed bunting and redpoll. The chough, rarest of all birds, has been seen in the Mawddach Estuary.

The gold in the estuary bed has been washed down over the centuries by the Mawddach and its tributaries from the hills north and east of Dolgellau. The land grants of the first Cymmer Abbey included "from the sea to Dolgellau, the mountains northwards and all the rivers, lakes and waters, all that flew above, and all beneath, minerals in the rocks and treasure in the ground".[8] The abbots dug for gold at Bontddu, close to the estuary, but of course lacked means to dredge the alluvial mud. The RTZ geologists who studied the tributaries draining eastward and southward into the Mawddach estuary reported that in nearly every case the panned concentrate showed "significant gold values". In April and May 1970, after putting a notice in the press, RTZ made a seismic refraction survey involving small charges of gelignite in the Mawddach Estuary.[9]

The Coed-y-Brenin forest, where RTZ hopes to mine copper ore, has suffered aesthetically from tracts of dark conifers sown by the Forestry Commission. Nevertheless there are fine patches of open hillside and oak forest; boisterous rivers in which the salmon and sea trout leap; and a "Precipice Walk" for those with a head for heights.

The waterfalls have excited visitors from the eighteenth century to William Condry who writes:

> Where the Cain flows into the Mawddach is a place of much delight, a place of roaring waters shadowed by oaks and rowans, a place of rocks, moss, ferns and slender St. John's wort; of buzzards, grey wagtails, pied fly-catchers and large wood ants scurrying about the gold-mine ruins.[10]

Much of the land round the RTZ site belongs to the Vaughans, one of the oldest families in the county. One modern visitor was told by an old man that,

> Many generations of the family had been tenants of the Vaughans. And long ago the Vaughans made use of the *droit de seigneur*——a phrase he did not use——by seducing young daughters of tenants and when objections were voiced eviction followed. A long time ago![11]

When the first afforestation was started after the First World War it was called Vaughan Forest, a name it kept until George V's Silver Jubilee when it became King's Forest, in Welsh——Coed-y-Brenin.

The present owner, Brigadier Vaughan, has allowed RTZ to explore for copper on his estate. The company first took an interest in this region after reading about the nineteenth-century "turf copper", which indicated bedrock mineralization. According to an RTZ report, field work started in May 1968, while two years before this RTZ had begun to negotiate with the owners of the mineral rights.[12] Diamond drilling began in January 1969.

The exploration subsidiary Riofinex Ltd. did not seek planning permission to drill. Later the company stated that "no application for planning permission to carry out exploratory drilling had been submitted before, because the applicants did not consider it necessary; nor did the planning authority. Subsequently the council changed its mind."[13] The question of whether planning permission was needed for exploratory drilling was later discussed at the Public Inquiry. But it seems that Merioneth County Council, far from saying that planning permission was not necessary, did not know that RTZ was there. The Park Planning Committee (which deals with that part of the

county that lies within the National Park) was informed of the RTZ
drilling in late 1969. According to John Lazarus, deputy planning
officer of Merioneth County Council:

> They'd been doing surreptitious drilling for two years before that.
> According to the book, development requires planning permission
> but it's not illegal unless an enforcement order has been served.
> What they were doing was enforceable but we never served an
> enforcement notice on them. We didn't know. They were drilling in
> the middle of the trees. It's only lately they've gone onto open
> land. We knew there was something going on in a vague sort of
> way. It's one of the facts of life here that people are always chip-
> ping away at bits of rock. . . . I understand that they drilled forty
> holes in those two years. . . . We had an application years ago for a
> chap doing geological work——we'd no idea he was from RTZ. He
> came up here and chipped at bits of stones. Later I myself came on
> a man drilling and asked him who he was working for and he said
> for some Irish people. I asked who were behind *them* and he said
> he didn't know. Then the word got around that it was RTZ and we
> had a bit of an up-and-downer with them before they put in their
> application. They said that exploration had to be clandestine, this
> was how mining worked, otherwise other people would come
> in. . . .[14]

As early as January 1970, RTZ was informed that permission was
required. In April it filed an application but meanwhile continued
drilling, sometimes keeping the drill-rigs running day and night and
seven days a week, causing annoyance to local residents. Since the
County Council refrained from issuing an enforcement order, RTZ
went on drilling until November 1970, when the Welsh Office asked
it to desist. The company agreed, although still maintaining its legal
right to drill. Friends of the Earth, however, claimed in the *Ecologist*
for June 1971:

> RTZ's contention that planning permission was not legally re-
> quired for this work seems no more than face-saving sophistry.
> RTZ's view of the law is not supported by the sources and auth-
> orities it has cited; is not shared by the Merioneth County Council,
> the Welsh Office, the Department of Trade and Industry, or our

own counsel; and is hard to reconcile with RTZ's request for prior permission for shallower and less extensive drilling in the open country of the Mawddach.

In the months before the Inquiry which began on 15 December 1970 RTZ made soothing noises, particularly with regard to the plans for the Mawddach Estuary. "It's only a gleam in the eye at the moment," said John Williams, the company s legal adviser, in September.[15] A few weeks later, Lord Byers, the RTZ director responsible for the project, went even further: "Personally I think the gold is a dead duck. But for the sake of £6,000——which is all it would cost to drill six bore holes——we think it is worth while finding out once and for all if there is any gold there."[16]

Soon afterwards, on 12 November 1970 the *New Scientist* carried an article by Jon Tinker, which greatly upset the company and alarmed British conservationists. Under the headline "Snowdonia cops it", the article asserted that:

Amid endless protestations of concern for the environment by a propaganda machine which has so far carried all before it, Rio Tinto-Zinc are preparing a £60 million opencast copper mine which may tear out 35 million tons of rock a year from the heart of one of Britain's most magnificent landscapes. . . . Presiding over the proposed despoliation will be Frank Byers, leader of the Liberal peers and RTZ's director in charge of exploration. Lord Byers regards himself as a conservationist: "I would loathe to see opencast mining in all our national parks", he told me over lunch in the RTZ boardroom recently. "But in two or three it would be OK," he added thoughtfully. . . . He promised that Rio Tinto would "cosmeticize" its opencast copper mine, and enthused on the miraculous abilities of modern earthmoving equipment. "All we shall do will be to create new mountains where there weren't any before", he said, explaining that you could build hills 600 ft tall from the tailings of unwanted rock and thereby hide the mine itself. He dismissed opposition as coming from a very few regrettably articulate people: "Hardly anyone ever goes there you know. The logical conclusion of their views is that no one should be allowed into a national park because they leave litter and destroy the solitude."

According to Tinker, Lord Byers repeated his doubts about the Mawddach Estuary plan. Tinker quoted him as saying: "We can go anywhere else in the world for our gold: so far as I am concerned you can have the Mawddach." At this point Tinker added a speculative comment that was to enrage RTZ:

> While it might be crediting RTZ with too Machiavellian a plan to suggest that they put up the Mawddach gold dredging only in order to abandon it later, it is hard not to see the advantages of such a ploy. RTZ would be able to pose as the magnanimous corporation refraining from ruining a beautiful and popular estuary and the county council would be able to take the credit for persuading it to do so. In the self-congratulatory conservationist haze which would envelop the subject, opencast coppermining could then be given a go-ahead.[17]*

One month later the *New Scientist* published Lord Byers's reply to what he called "straight misrepresentation and journalistic inventions" in Tinker's article. Of the statements attributed to him by Tinker, Lord Byers denied only one——that he would "loathe to see opencast mining in all national parks but in two or three it would be OK". This was a fabrication, Lord Byers protested. Moreover he denied the imputation that "he dismissed opposition as coming from a very few regrettably articulate people".

The *New Scientist* article alerted Merioneth to the possibility of a mine, and polarized both sides before the impending Inquiry.

The main supporter of RTZ was the Government in Whitehall. Imports of copper cost Britain about £100 million a year to the detriment of her balance of payments. Moreover much of this metal comes from countries like Chile and Zambia which might prove politically "unstable". According to Lord Byers, exploration for minerals in the United Kingdom had been encouraged by Wilson's Government as well as by the Conservatives.

The Merioneth National Farmers Union favours both RTZ schemes. The county secretary, Douglas Williams, told me that "Coed-y-Brenin is very poor soil, much of it just rock outcrop and only good for grazing or forestry. It's very wild. It's beautiful but

* As this book was going to press, in March 1972, RTZ announced the abandonment of the Mawddach gold project.

there's not many people that go there walking." He thought the
Mawddach Estuary scheme would improve the area between Dolgellau and the first bridge: "Even people of my age can remember
when there was threshing and farming there. Now it's a tidal marsh.
If they dredge, it will improve the flooded areas above the first
bridge. It's all flooded now with wild duck and so on. . . ."[18] Many
NFU members allowed RTZ to drill on their land and were paid handsome "disturbance money".

Many shopkeepers, hoteliers, small businessmen and artisans believed and still believe that RTZ would bring work and wealth to the
neighbourhood. Their views are summed up by Dolgellau Rural District Council, which favours the company's plans. The clerk to the
council, Bryn Williams-Jones, was eloquent about the proposed mine.
First, there was the question of jobs. RTZ had given the council to
understand that the copper project "would require 1000 to 1500
people to open it up, thereafter 500 men, which from our point of
view means 500 families". The estuary project would require about
40 people: "They told us that they'd be able to recruit almost all the
labour locally either in the county or just outside. . . . They went to
great pains to indicate that they would initiate training schemes for
school leavers. We wouldn't tie them down to that, but we've no
doubt that they would back it up."

However, Williams-Jones emphasized that the problem facing the
region was not so much unemployment as depopulation:

> During the last sixteen years we've lost 34 percent of the people in
> this Rural District Council area, or if you like south-west Mer-
> ioneth. This aspect of depopulation is never referred to by people
> when they talk of unemployment. We're fast approaching the posi-
> tion when South Merioneth will no longer be economically viable,
> [when] we won't be able to support and maintain the public ser-
> vices we've got in terms of the responsibilities and needs we are
> called to face. This is an area that suffers, I use the word advisedly,
> from a great influx of tourists each year. But the contribution they
> make to the economy of the area is virtually nil. Others would
> dispute this. But to take one example, we have to provide a sewer-
> age scheme for a small village community. When this was first
> mooted it was going to cost £27,000. When it was implemented

and the scheme expanded to take in the needs of the tourist population, it cost us £250,000. Five-sixths of this scheme is idle for nine months of the year. One result is that we're the highest rated RDC in the UK. The rate burden as such has to be met by the local rate-payer. Industrial property accounts for less than 2 percent of rateable resources. It follows that the major burden of rate falls on domestic rate-payers. We need population and development.... We are obviously a receiving authority in terms of exchequer grants. If we increase our population, the government contribution will be so much more. During the last two years we lost 10 percent of our rateable resources when a military camp was closed down. But we also lost a substantial part of our population. This smaller population has to meet an ever increasing rate burden. The position is getting worse. We consider that on the principle "the Lord giveth, the Lord taketh away", the government has a moral responsibility to do something about it. They came [to the military camp] in the mid-thirties and left without a by-your-leave in the 60s. Had this happened in any other comparable area, what repercussions there would have been! They made a tremendous fuss about unemployment in the north-east and within a few weeks the government had appointed a special minister with plenary powers. [Lord Hailsham in 1963.] Had it been an area with the figures I've been giving you, it would have required the presence not of one minister but of the whole cabinet.... If the government's not going to do anything about it, we'll have to look elsewhere and the answer lies in people like Rio Tinto who are big enough in capital and prestige to do something about the position with which we are faced.... Far too many people are suffering from the "light industry syndrome" as a cure to all our ills. What we get is a lot of semi-bankrupt businessmen from the Midlands who take advantage of a grant and then skittle off back to the Midlands. What we want is an industry that is not faced by one financial crisis after another.... All that we've been concerned with so far is the principle of the thing. We haven't got down to the vulgar details.... And how do we tie this up with our status as a national park? My council's view is that far too much is made of national parks as such. The area involved in the copper mining is three or four square miles compared with a total of 800 or so [actually 845]. We've got to put the thing in its proper perspective. There are far too many people who think of a national park as their private property. They think that they own the whole damned place. They've made their pile in the Midlands. They've come here to live and "I'm all right, Jack!". The fact is that people do live in a national park. They're entitled as much as anyone else to opportunities for advancement. After all, we're living in a very material world, aren't we? We're not immune to the trends to affluence——nor the trends to permissiveness. Whether it's right or wrong is not the point. It's a question of survival. I don't see how you are going to survive by going against the main stream. I don't see how you can justify the view that national parks should be a nature reserve for ramblers and that sort of people. They think it should be a game reservation like Tanganyika or somewhere. But *I'm* not prepared to act the noble savage.[19]

The main political parties in Merioneth favour mining development in the county. The Labour MP Will Edwards said in September 1970, a fortnight before Tinker's *New Scientist* article:

It is inconceivable to think of dredging in that beautiful estuary. But if it is to be a conservation area and we cannot develop there, *we must have something in return in the way of amenities and jobs* [italics added]. . . . The hill area is sterile. Mining there would provide about 300 jobs, more than dredging for gold.

However, he said that the copper should be extracted by deep, not opencast mining.[20] The Merioneth Conservatives, who command support from shopkeepers and owners of mineral rights, are broadly favourable to the RTZ copper project. The Plaid Cymru, or Welsh Nationalist Party, is weak in Merioneth but is believed to be in favour of RTZ. It is noted with satisfaction that RTZ has appointed Welsh-speaking executives to Anglesey Aluminium company, and has given a bardic Chair, as prize, to Merioneth Young Farmers Eisteddfod.

However, it would be wrong to infer that all Merioneth favours a mine while opposition comes only from outsiders and English people. The County Planning Officer, the County Planning Committee and the County Council itself were all opposed to the plan from the start. Most of the tenant farmers round Coed-y-Brenin feared getting displaced by the mine. Local anglers feared that either the mine or the dredge might spoil the fishing. People living along the estuary were almost unanimous in opposing the mine. Nor should it be thought that opposition came only from middle-class, English people. There is a general fear that if a mine is opened, Irishmen will be brought in to do the construction work. The county is named after Meirion, son of Cunedda, who was given this region 1500 years ago "for ridding the land of the Irish".*[21]

Behind the local resisters to RTZ were outside bodies such as the Ramblers Association, the Youth Hostels Association, the National Trust and the Council for the Protection of Rural Wales. The last named had recently gained new gusto from the adherence of Wynford Vaughan Thomas, a famous radio broadcaster during the war and still a national figure in his native Wales. He is contemptuous of the arguments used to justify the copper mine: "It's the old story of Rhodes buying the Boer farmers by offering them an ox wagon——except that now it's a Rolls-Royce. ... The shopkeepers think they're going to profit from the mine and the miners think they'll be able to go to Dolgellau for a dirty weekend. What a surprise they've got coming to them! Do you know Dolgellau? It's the only inhabited piece of scree in Great Britain."[22] I hasten to add that Vaughan-Thomas did not intend these remarks to be taken too seriously.

When the Inquiry began at Dolgellau on 15 December 1970, it soon became clear that the two sides were talking at cross-purposes. The applicants, RTZ, wished to confine the arguments to the effects of exploratory drilling. Their opponents wished to discuss the likely effects of the mine and the dredge. They argued that if permission was given for exploratory drilling, it would be virtually impossible to turn round later and to refuse mining permission.

However RTZ's spokesmen insisted that "as a matter of law the present applications must be considered in their own terms and on their own merits".[23] Exploratory drilling, they claimed, would not be an annoyance, and rigs on the Mawddach Estuary would not

* Critics of RTZ in North Wales say that most of the jobs at Anglesey Aluminium have gone to Irishmen. This story is often repeated on Holyhead itself. My inquiries there suggest that the story is almost totally unfounded.

"generate more noise or exhaust than an agricultural tractor". The sulphides brought to the surface by drilling on Coed-y-Brenin would not be dangerous to the streams nearby, while the noise would be less than that of the present forestry work. The exploration drilling was a commercial operation but "it would be in the national interest" to carry it out:

> The advantage to be gained, not only by the applicants but by the nation as a whole, in furthering the geological knowledge of the area would seem to far outweigh any possible argument that these operations ought not to be permitted for amenity reasons.

The counsel for the company reached a fine peroration of injured innocence:

> The applicants had not painted rosy pictures. They said, instead, that there was no more than a hundred to one chance of finding gold in the Mawddach Estuary and copper in the Coed-y-Brenin Forest. . . . The rush to judgement pursued by the objectors was unnecessary; they could not possibly know what was actually intended as the applicants themselves did not yet know. . . . If no gold or copper was found there would be no exploitation so how did the present applications prejudge any future proposals?

This question was answered repeatedly by various objectors. Their principal spokesman, the County Planning Officer, stated that he himself had originally been in favour of both applications, seeing them as an opportunity to gain knowledge of the geology of the National Park, as well as providing jobs for the unemployed. Later

> he considered that he was mistaken in his former view because the application to explore could not be considered in isolation from the very substantial development which would follow if the exploration was successful. . . . The applications for exploration and exploitation were merely different stages of one development and were inextricably joined. Even if exploration proved that there were no minerals present in sufficient quantity to make their extraction profitable now, there might come a time when extraction did become profitable. The threat of this kind of exploration would be a Sword of Damocles hanging over the planning authority's head and the heads of the residents.

The Mawddach Association, representing 273 objectors, most of whom lived by the Estuary, were still more vehement on this point. They conceded RTZ's case that preliminary investigation would do little harm to the estuary, but insisted that "licences to explore . . . were in reality licences to exploit". It was perfectly possible to decide in principle, then and now, if there should be industrial development on the Mawddach Estuary.

While RTZ stuck to discussing the exploration only, objectors at the Inquiry insisted on a debate about the likely effect of exploitation. The Planning Officer declared that a successful drilling operation, carried out with Government permission, would set the stage for full-scale, open-cast mining: "This could only mean the practical abandonment of the National Park concept. If one of the most famous beauty spots in the National Park were opened to industrial exploitation . . . tourism over a much wider area would be prejudiced." The devastation caused by earlier extractive works had made two large parts of the county unpleasant and dangerous for their residents. The boundaries of the National Park had had to be altered to exclude the ruined slate quarries of Blaenau Ffestiniog. Caernarvon, the neighbouring county, was thinking of spending £150,000 to try to convert old quarries into parks, but the planning officer warned that "remedial work would only be cosmetic. The bones of the ancient devastation would almost certainly be exposed."

It was important to appreciate, said the County Planning Officer, that as the coast was increasingly used for tourists wanting gregarious holidays, so the rivers and estuaries of Wales would be still more important to people in search of privacy. If the exploration by RTZ was successful and led to exploitation, this would encourage applicants to explore and exploit the other minerals known to exist in the National Park.

Although RTZ had claimed only a one-in-a-hundred chance of successful exploration, their local supporters spoke hopefully of the benefits from a mine. The spokesman for Dolgellau Rural District Council voices its belief in "heavy industry based on the natural resources of the area". Even RTZ did not keep to its own terms of reference but, by implication, preached the benefits of mineral exploitation:

On the one hand the National Park included a resident population (some retired, some finding their living there) and, on the
other hand, the flora and fauna. But in the end it was the people
who mattered. If all was well with the economic life of the area,
the applicants might understand being told to go away but this
was far from being so. The situation was one of unarrested depopulation; lack of employment opportunities; and a poor state of
agriculture. Tourism offered mainly seasonal employment and because of that there was all year round unemployment. Attempts to
establish new industry had been quite ineffective.

When the Inquiry Inspector had listened to evidence from the
public bodies concerned in the debate, various individuals were in-
vited to state their opinion. Among those who spoke in favour of RTZ
was Brigadier Vaughan who owns the mineral rights for much of the
Coed-y-Brenin site. Life in this area was grim, he said, and so it was
sane to investigate whether the county had minerals which could
lead to its future prosperity. Another speaker, T. M. Roberts, who
lived at Penmaenpool on the Mawddach Estuary, supported the
dredging plan on the grounds that "the noise and smoke produced
would be nothing compared with the fumes of increasing road traffic
and the noise of low-flying aircraft".

Important evidence was given by Cyril J. Jones, a tenant farmer
and employee of the Forestry Commission, who lives on the site of
the proposed copper mine. From two years' experience of the drilling
teams, some of whom have worked on his farm, Jones "was convinced that the applicants knew the potential of this area without
any further drilling. It was only a matter of time before they would
need permission to mine. If such permission was granted he would
have to leave his home, his farm and possibly the Forestry Commission by whom he had been employed for 31 years." Nearly a year
after giving evidence at the Inquiry, Jones was keeping up his resistance to the proposal for a mine. However, he said: "We're trying to
fight a £320 million company. And all the money I spend I have to
find out of my own pocket. I spent a week at the Public Inquiry but
got no recompense for it. . . . They're a great psychological company,
RTZ. Even before the *New Scientist* article, I and others suspected
that the Mawddach gold was a diversion. At the Inquiry the company

didn't seem to know what kind of dredge would be needed or even if it would be obtainable. . . . The Hermon Valley will be finished. I'm a conservationist, I always have been but I think in 20 years our vote will be useless because there won't be anything left to conserve."[24]

Seven months passed between the Public Inquiry and the decision by the Government to allow exploration. During this time, the objectors to RTZ continued their protests through the press and public meetings. The company used its far greater financial resources to advertise its own arguments. At the annual general meeting of RTZ held on 19 May 1971 Sir Val Duncan devoted much of his speech to his "concern with the environment". This passage was reprinted as an advertisement in many national newspapers, presumably at the cost of many thousands of pounds. For example, the full-page advertisement in the *Daily Mail* of 21 May 1971 shows the faces of smiling, multi-racial RTZ workers under a block of text headlined "Natural resource companies have special responsibility . . . not to destroy the environment". These are some of the points made by Sir Val in the advertisement:

> However, no change means no development, no growing opportunity for a better life for the poor, the less fortunate throughout the world. Picking at random some examples within the RTZ Group where environmental considerations have weighed very heavily in the construction and operation of our major activities, I might mention Lornex in British Columbia . . . US Borax . . . [and] Palabora, our copper complex situated next to the Kruger National Park in South Africa, where it is acknowledged by experts that wild life which abounds in the immediate environment of the main plant. Indeed a family of hippos has taken up permanent residence in the tailings dam!

It should be remarked that the Palabora mine lies *outside* the Kruger National Park while the Coed-y-Brenin site lies *inside* the Snowdonia National Park, which is only a tenth the size of Kruger. Moreover the other mines that Sir Val selected "at random" are in Canada and the United States where the conservationist movement is strong and has forced industrialists to control pollution. Perhaps it is a pity that Sir Val's selection "at random" did not light on the Bristol and Anglesey smelters, or on Bougainville, which was, but no longer is, a peaceful and beautiful island.

On 15 July 1971 the Welsh Office approved RTZ's applications for planning permission for mineral exploration at Coed-y-Brenin and in the Mawddach Estuary. At about the same time, RTZ announced that in conjunction with six other companies, it had set up and financed an unofficial commission to inquire how mining could be harmonized with our National Parks. The Commission was headed by Lord Zuckerman, a scientist who began his career doing research into the social life of apes, later becoming Scientific Adviser to the Cabinet Office, chairman of the Manpower Committee and Chief Scientific Adviser to the Minister of Defence——among many important posts in a distinguished career. When asked by the *Observer* about his committee on National Parks and mining, Lord Zuckerman said: "I don't want to speak about it. And I certainly don't want to speak to you." The Council for the Preservation of Rural England called it a "whitewash" and later refused to give evidence on the grounds that it had been set up "unilaterally" by the industry.

On 10 November 1971 a Mineral Exploration Bill was given an unopposed Second Reading. The Bill sets aside £50 million to pay 35 percent of the cost of looking for and mining non-ferrous metals. The miners pay back the Government if they make a successful strike. The Minister for Industry, Sir John Eden, told the Commons:

> At present we import annually over £600 millions worth of non-ferrous metals and their ores. If we can foster the revival of a healthy and prosperous mining industry in this country, we can achieve significant savings in foreign exchange, establish secure sources of supply, and create new wealth.[25]

Wealth, or Mammon as it was once called, is worshipped still. In the interests of "growth", or greed, the metals are ripped from the earth to be used in motor cars, Concorde aeroplanes, beer cans, nuclear weapons and TV sets. Instead of conserving the world's dwindling natural resources, Governments encourage the miners to still more frantic efforts. As a consequence of this mineral rush, farmers are thrown off their land; whole mountains are scooped away and their poisons dumped in the sea; industry invades the few last patches of natural beauty. The poet Robert Graves has called on the

Welsh Gods to put a curse on the heads of the company that wants to mine in Gwynnedd. In ancient Germany it was the Gods who died for stealing the gold from the Rhine. The prophecy of Paul Kruger should not be ignored: "Every ounce of gold taken from the bowels of our soil will yet have to be weighed against rivers of tears."

NOTES

1. *Observer*, 3–11–71.
2. *Irish Times*, 21–1–71.
3. William Condry, *The Snowdonia National Park*, p. 12.
4. *Guardian*, 27–10–71.
5. Michael Wharton, who writes the column, in conversation with author.
6. Condry, 56–7.
7. *A Topographical Dictionary of Wales* (published 1833).
8. Jessica Lofthouse, *North Wales for the Countrygoer* (Hale 1970), p. 116.
9. Public Inquiry at Dolgellau, December 1970. Inspector's report, para. 35.
10. Condry, p. 225.
11. Lofthouse, pp. 114–15.
12. *Observer*.
13. Inspector's Report, para. 83.
14. Interview with author.
15. *Sunday Times*, 27–9–70.
16. *Sunday Times*, 18–10–70.
17. *New Scientist*, 12–11–70.
18. Interview with author.
19. Interview with author.
20. *Sunday Times*, 27–9–70.
21. Lofthouse, p. 25.
22. Conversation with author.
23. The following account is from the report of the Inspector at the Inquiry.
24. Interview with author.
25. *Times*, 11–11–71.

APPENDIX A

"Comalco's Capital Coup" by Dr. A. R. Hall of the Australian National University (reproduced by kind permission of the Australian Financial Review).

The practice of selling off a minority interest in a company when its earning rate is high, when the share market is receptive, and in a proportion such that the new public security has considerable scarcity value, is almost as old as the company form of organization itself.

When it is practised by local companies on local investors, apart from its contribution to the profits of underwriting firms and jobbing stags, perhaps its main immediate economic effect is to increase the inequality of the domestic income distribution.

When the same device is used to give a local flavour to an overseas-controlled firm, especially if it takes the form of an issue with a high share premium element, the economic consequences for the domestic economy are more disturbing. A case in point, though not the only one, is the Comalco new issue made last April.

Its entry to the market created a political stir. Was the company's then apparent lack of political nous a clever device for distracting attention from the lack of benefit which this issue contributed to the Australian economy? Were the eminent politicians who refused the company's friendly advances not merely properly upright citizens, but sceptics of the real benefits of the company's offer to the Australian economy?

That it was of benefit to the company is not being questioned. Nor are the benefits to the friends of the company who took up the issue, and to the clients of the underwriting broker, seriously in doubt. Their immediate, and still available, capital gain may be sufficient to offset the low earnings yield which they are receiving and which they are likely to receive for some time.

Whether this statement is correct or not deserves serious examination by the underwriting brokers but is not my immediate concern.

What worries me is the conflict between the possible gain of selected private investors and the national loss through the misallocation of scarce Australian risk capital which this type of operation makes possible.

Attention will also be drawn to the fact that this device results in a high earnings yield on overseas investments; one which will, accordingly, become a further contributing factor to the current disturbingly high rate of growth of aggregate overseas dividend and interest payments.

Comalco's directors may be genuinely concerned, as they claim to be in their last annual report, to limit the company's contribution to environmental pollution. It is a pity that they did not show the same regard for the best use of a different type of Australian resource——its scarce supply of local risk capital.

Let us consider what they have achieved in this area. To do so properly we need to examine not the just-released accounts for the year ending 31 December 1970 but a rough approximation to what Comalco's shareholders' funds account will look like on 31 December 1971. This is so because their second bite at Australian (and New Zealand) supplies of risk capital, amounting to somewhat more than $13·6m, is due to be made during the next few weeks.

To move from the 1970 to the 1971 statement of shareholders' funds it has been assumed that the 1970 rate of profit will be maintained and that the prospectus intention, observed in 1970, to retain about 55 percent of net profits will continue to be realized. The validity of our basic argument will not be significantly affected by the likely actual variations from these assumptions.

When the required arithmetic is done it would appear that Comalco's net profit in 1971 will be about $20m and its 1971 end-year shareholders' fund about $131m. The substantial accuracy of this estimate may be judged from the elements of which it is composed,

	$ '000
Shareholders funds at 31/3/70	106,540
Receipts from call on Australian and New Zealand shareholders, 31/3/71	13,649
Retained profits during 1971	11,000
	131,189

The next step is to determine the proportion of total shareholders' funds at the end of 1971 that can properly be attributed to Australian and New Zealand shareholders. The steps in this estimate are:

New issue 1/5/70	22·1
Share of retained earnings for eight months of 1970	2·2
"Australian" equity at 21/12/70	24·3
Share of retained earnings for 1971	3·7
Call 31/3/71	13·6
Share of retained earnings accruing on call	1·6
Total Australian (and New Zealand) provision of equity funds at 31/12/71	43·2

When the $43·2m is compared with the expected 1971 total of shareholders' funds it will be apparent that Australian and New Zealand shareholders will have contributed almost one third of Comalco's equity funds.

Now consider what these shareholders are entitled to receive. Their legal equity in the company is not in proportion to the funds actually supplied but to paid-up capital which appears in the company's books not as about one-third but as exactly one-tenth.

So if Comalco earns £20m in 1971 the Australians' and New Zealanders' legal share of it will be 10 percent or $2m. The rate of return of the shareholders' funds which they will have supplied will be about 4·6 percent.

Compare the return of CRA and Kaiser Aluminium, who share equally in the remaining 90 percent of earnings. Their equity funds supplied on 31 December 1971, will amount to about $88m, their share in net profits $18m, their rate of return 20·4 percent.

There are qualifications to this enormous earnings yield

differential. Dividend payments to A shareholders (the public) are expected to be made from tax free funds so that the after tax dividend yield is not as low as it appears, at least for investors subject to the upper levels of the marginal rate of income tax.

The Australian minority shareholders in CRA will get their small cut from CRA's inflated Comalco earnings. These shareholders, with Comalco's friends, have also received the capital gains sugar on the Comalco pill. But these are essentially minor qualifications.

And now for the final irony of this "Australian" company. Perhaps some mute, inglorious Australian shareholder will be provoked by this analysis to suggest to his representative director at the company's annual meeting on Friday that a partial remedy for the inequity involved would be that the share premium supplied by A shareholders should be converted entirely into fully paid A shares which would then rank equally with B and C shares.

Before he takes such action he should examine carefully the sections of the prospectus which define the powers of his single representative on the board. He will discover that in return for about one-third of the equity he has obtained not merely only one-tenth of the paid-up capital but zero control over the company's affairs.

For all practical purposes his director holds a sinecure with the responsibilities and powers that one associates with that type of office.

The conclusions are inescapable: a minority interest gives no significant control over company policy. In the Comalco affair, and others like it, scarce Australian equity funds are condemned to receive a much lower earnings yield than could be obtained elsewhere on Australian controlled equity issues.

Real domestic national product is henceforth lower than it would have been if Comalco and Co. had been given a cold shoulder. Yet another burden has been placed on the Australian balance of payments. It is obviously important that the share market mechanics of this type of operation should be clearly understood. Because the market is traditionally biased in favour of "glamour" names——because it was, at the time of the issue, valuing many major mining concerns at rates of discount that were extremely optimistic and because it was believed that the issue was a good thing——it was also believed (and subsequently confirmed) that the share market would value the relatively few Comalco shares offered at a price greater than the issue price.

Faced with the prospect of an immediate capital gain how many individual private investors were likely to ignore one of Australia's leading underwriting broker's "no hesitation in recommending" such an issue even though some of the more well informed among them may have recognized that it was not in Australia's interest to be party to such a deal? Comalco's likely defence that it was simply "meeting the market" may be genuine and one can hardly blame its management for doing its best for its overseas owners. But we should note carefully that the market it is "meeting" is far removed from that perfectly competitive market which might conceivably justify such actions.

It is much more correct to say that they were taking full advantage of the imperfections of the Australian share market, presumably on the advice of their Australian underwriting brokers.

If the Comalco affair induces Australians to fear the British, the Americans and others when they come bearing minority interest gifts then perhaps the price of this case may not be excessive in the long run.

The market has proved itself incapable of judging the national merits of the sale of minority interests. Left to itself it is more than likely that it will repeat the error. Given this demonstrated failure of the market mechanism there is no further excuse for the Government not to face the issues involved in the control of overseas investment.

The available alternatives have become clear. Either no minority interest at all and control through taxation and other measures or an insistence on majority Australian control.

From the national point of view, if not from that of a few favoured individuals, overseas controlled minority interests should be avoided.

Printed by Leo Thorpe Ltd., Wembley.